Jeannine,
Thanks for
taking the journey.
See you in
Kauai —
Love + Joy
Patrick Feren

The Memoir of the
Little Man

Finding the Prince in the Ashes of Chaos, Dysfunction, and Mental Illness.

Y0-DOI-540

by Patrick Feren

Copyright © 2023 Patrick Feren

All rights reserved

No part of this publication may be reproduced in any form or by any means, electronic or mechanical, including photocopying, recording, or by any information storage and retrieval system, without permission in writing from the publisher. Reviewers may quote brief passages.

Cover Design and Interior Layout by: Jonathan Zenz

Published in the United States of America

Developmental & Substantive Editor
Rita Andriello-Feren

Proofreader
Sue Buckley

Disclaimer: The names and identifying details of some characters and events in this book have been changed to protect the privacy of the individuals and their descendants. Also, some characters might appear as composite characters representing a single person.

I am dedicating this book to my best friend, wife, lover, partner, and creative genius, Rita Andriello-Feren. I am truly blessed to have you on this incredible adventure with me.

Acknowledgments

Everyone we meet and every experience we have shapes our lives. I am grateful for the many people who have assisted me in shaping my life and, in turn, assisted me with the birth of *The Memoir of the Little Man*. I feel as though I have had many lives within this lifetime. It would be impossible to remember and name all of those who have touched my life and this memoir, but I have done my best.

I am grateful for my mother, father, and brother who dominate the pages of this book. The good, the bad, and the ugly of our experiences together made me the person I am today. Would I have preferred to bypass the trauma of our life together? Of course I would have, and yet, because of all these experiences, I learned what I did not want to be. As I have moved forward with my life, I believe I have made healthier choices.

I thank my Nana who welcomed us into her home on many of those frightening nights when we sought safety.

I am grateful for my religious training as a young Catholic boy. Although I did not remain a Catholic, that training birthed my faith in the invisible. I will never forget the hope and peace those Saints and Heavenly Father gave to a scared and confused boy who had nowhere to go for help.

I am in deep gratitude for those teachers who recognized my true potential beyond my confusion and fear. Thank you for fostering my gifts and talents and giving me a place to express myself fully.

I am also grateful for my fellow students at St. David's who were my family away from home. Those friendships and connections became the perfect respite from my traumatic home life.

I am filled with gratitude for all the insights I have gained from the Science of Mind teachings. Dr. Ernest Holmes, its Founder, synthesized the best of all faiths and found a way to explain it simply. Because of Dr. Holmes and the long New Thought lineage before him, I have come to recognize the Divine within myself which has always reflected Itself as my deep intuition. I also understand that I am always at choice as to how I react to my circumstances. I know it is my intuition and the power of choice that guided me through the turbulent times of my childhood, my recovery, and continues to guide me always.

Thank you to my first therapist, Paul, and his gentle yet powerful guidance. It was under his care that I started to discover and release the curiosity and confusion of my childhood. My gratitude goes beyond words.

I am blessed to have had spiritual teachers and mentors on my road to becoming my true self and the New Thought Minister I am today. There were my first Science of Mind teachers: Richard Morgan RScP and Rev. Dr. Marlene Morris. I thank them for recognizing my spiritual potential and for being dear friends. Thank you to my dear friend, Dr. James Mellon, who truly is the teacher of teachers. If I ever doubted that I was God, he wiped that doubt away.

A special acknowledgment to Sue Buckley and all her special talents, one of them being the master proofreader of this book. Thank you, Sue, not only for your expertise, but for all the heart you put into your work on this book.

Thank you, Rev. Dr. Jonathan Zenz, who is responsible for

the layout and cover design of this book. Thank you for your creativity, your love, support, and friendship.

Mahalo nui loa to my Center for Spiritual Living Kaua'i family who supported the idea and manifestation of *The Memoir of the Little Man* by reminding me to get it done so they could experience it.

I am blessed and grateful for my wife, Rita. She has always nurtured and loved the "all of me," giving me the strength to write this book. I have openly shared the experience of my childhood with her throughout our 25 years together. Her ability to cut through to the essence of my deepest thoughts and emotions has enabled me to have the best editor a writer could want. Thank you, Rita, for your unconditional love that has allowed me to be so vulnerable and transparent in this memoir.

Last, but not least, I am deeply grateful to my inner child/Patrick and his incredible courage in navigating a turbulent childhood. I thank him for his innate knowing that life is to be treasured. His ability to stay positive enabled him to find the gift in it all. I am so proud of this Little Man who has become a beautiful, sensitive, and loving person. We did it Little Patrick! I love you!

PATRICK

Testimonials

"I am honored to review my spiritual brother's powerful memoir. Reading it was like riding a rollercoaster. Patrick's book is an authentic telling of his journey of turmoil and redemption. I feel like I know and better understand not only Patrick, but anyone who has come through trauma. The Memoir of the Little Man, at times, moved me to tears, made me smile, and opened my heart in a way that is difficult to describe. What I do know is that the reader will be affected in some deep way by this extraordinarily strong and courageous man's words."
-Sue Buckley, Friend and Spiritual Sister

"In my career as a Foster Care/Adoptions Social Worker & LMFT, I have seen first-hand, how the trauma of abuse, both verbal & physical can impact a young child's life emotionally & developmentally. In The Memoir of the Little Man, Patrick Feren pulls back the curtain of his own 'horror story' of childhood & shares with us just how devastating an experience it can be. From his first intuition that he was to be the 'protector' of his mother & family as a very young boy, he shares how he was able to navigate unimaginable situations & still survive to become the man he is today. In his search for answers, he discovers the reasons for many reactions & reasons abused adults often experience such as anxiety, fear, & hypervigilance. He has researched & found resources to help explain & support his journey. This book has been written with much truth, passion, & honesty & will help anyone looking to start their own Inner Child healing."
-Dana Craig Baier, Foster Care/ Adoptions Social Worker & LMFT

"Patrick Feren's The Memoir of the Little Man is a must read for all those who have had a dysfunctional childhood or have mental illness in their family history. Patrick writes with clarity and depth about his life both as a child and young man. He provides coping tools and lots of hope as he grows up to be a highly functioning man who is thriving and helping hundreds of others. I highly recommend this compelling memoir!"
-Debra Valentina, Holistic Coach, Workshop Facilitator,
International Best-selling Author

"They say that books come along in life at the very moment they are needed in the world. I don't know if that's true, but I do know that it's true of this book. The Memoir of a Little Man *is an exquisite telling of the extraordinary life of a man who not only survived a challenging world but who used his experience to change that world and the people in it. Patrick's story is one that needs to be heard. His optimism, courage and wisdom will help and assist those on this ever changing planet for years to come."*

-Dr. James Mellon, Founding Spiritual Director of the Global Truth Center

"This is not just a book, but a powerful tool that underlines the importance of reconnecting with one's inner child, a topic that often gets overlooked in today's day and age.*

Its pages are packed with valuable insights into the process of acknowledging past wounds and embracing them, ways to love yourself, to nurture the child within, and to heal with kindness and understanding.

What struck me the most about The Memoir of the Little Man *is its emphasis on facing the past in order to move forward. Patrick, the author, encourages the readers to confront and accept their past, not as burdensome moments, but as a source of strength and wisdom.*

This book is a gift to anyone who has experienced the long-lasting effects of childhood trauma and seeks a guided path to recovery."

-Oleg Lougheed, Executive Director of Overcoming Odds

"Here is a bold masterpiece, a 'Boot Camp' for the soul that liberates anyone who believes that a horrific childhood is reason to grow up damaged.*

Patrick, his Mom's LITTLE MAN, responded to the extreme emotional abuse from his father by building a lasting inner citadel, not of hatred, but of the invaluable life skills of survival speech, acquiescence when prudent, amazing bravery and profound resilience.

As Patrick matured he chose not the role of victim but that of a SUPER HERO which catapulted him into his current MAGNIFICENT BIG MAN identity as Minister and Spiritual Director of Kauai's Center for Spiritual Living. In my eyes Rev. Patrick is a super evolved and highly valued role model and a very humane human being."

-Carole Rae Watanabe, artist and author of the Ecstatic Marriage of Life and Art

"I've always been interested in learning and researching the views of others whom have also grown up in a dysfunctional family setting.

Following the reading of The Memoir of the Little Man, it helped me to see that a human can have both the overwhelming love for a parent AND at the same time the wonderment of why that same parent would let the abuse continue in the household.

Mental health is a continual learning experience. How a child sees and feels the effects of the dysfunction in the family and ultimately how this child grows and adjusts to everyday life while tending their emotions with constant turmoil in the background, leads to the question of one's own stability and outlook on life.

The author's coping technique of 're-framing, re-claiming, and re-naming' the traumatic events is a wonderful healing technique.

The writer is truly inspiring! To grow up with the everyday traumatic events throughout the childhood years but to continue to have a positive and humorous outlook on life....is MAGNIFICENT!

-Wendy White, Life-long Friend

"Patrick Feren walks his talk. It could have been very easy to write a memoir for the purpose of justifying the horrors of a dysfunctional past and seeking sympathy, but this is not what is uncovered in The Memoir of the Little Man. Instead we are taken on a journey of dysfunction and dis-ease with deft guidance toward healing. At its core Patrick has authentically and eloquently shown that healing is assured when we have a willingness to truly do the work. It doesn't matter one's age, the distance or nearness of traumatic events, or the belligerence of relationships involved. Healing is an inside job of self-discovery. I am certain that anyone who reads this memoir will find healing in their own lives."

-Rev. Dr. Jonathan Zenz, Spiritual Director of Unity of Tucson

The Memoir of the Little Man *offers a reflection — a mirror image — of someone we know personally, and provides intimate insights into how Patrick Feren became the humorous, deeply feeling and insightful person he is today. His book is both a brave and sometimes bracing account of his childhood, and equally a testimonial to his maturation, crisis of conscience, and triumph of authenticity and naked truth that brought him to reconcile the lives of his father, his family and his person.*

We recommend this book to those of us who have experienced trauma, particularly in our early lives, which is probably mostly everyone, if not all of us. The book also presents some fascinating philosophical and spiritual investigations into how we are formed from the very beginning -- literally in utero -- and how these defenses play out in our growing years."

Laura Kaibel MA, Head Special Education Teacher

The Memoir of the Little Man *reveals the intricacies, challenges and rewards of human relationships that we can only begin to make sense of upon reflection and examination of our personal history. We each have our own unique story as we journey through life and I was drawn into the compelling truth with which Patrick shares his life. This is a touching story, and a deeply revealing expository account about how one negotiates life's obstacles and succeeds."*

David Pavlosky, Adjunct Assistant Professor • he/him/his Hunter College

Table of Contents

Foreword

Kaua`i is my favorite Hawaiian island by far. I've visited eight times now! In 2014, I had been a licensed spiritual practitioner for three years, and as I contemplated my upcoming trip to the island, I was resigned to missing a week of spiritual community. I knew Kaua`i didn't host a CSL. For the heck of it, though, I Googled "Centers for Spiritual Living, Kaua`i," hoping to be re-directed to a Unity or Universalist church on the island. *"Oh, my God!"* I shouted. *"Kaua`i has a CSL now! Look, it has a web page and everything!"*

This was my introduction nine years ago this month to Reverend Patrick Feren. I was captivated when I attended the service in June 2014 at the Aston Aloha Beach Hotel in Wailua, co-led by Rev. Patrick and his dynamic, smiling wife, Rev. Rita. What I learned about them astounded me. They were former actors and performers. That made sense based on their energy and fearlessness. They graduated from ministerial school together and were licensed and ordained as Center for Spiritual Living ministers. Check. But then I learned that Kaua`i was their first ministerial gig. Wait. What? No CSL minister does that! Yes, they had staff positions at the NoHo Arts Center for New Thought for a short time, but the concept of obtaining your ministerial license and then venturing out and starting your own spiritual center, well, that just wasn't done.

Nine years have passed since I met Rev. Patrick, and I can sincerely say I love this man. After reading *The Memoir of the Little Man*, I love him even more. I can now see that

i

the courage, openness, and faith he and his wife embodied to strike out on their own and spiritually pioneer Kaua`i parallels the survival and "thrival" skills he demonstrated as The Little Man.

I knew little about Rev. Patrick's background—he was an actor, made a living wearing Spiderman spandex for several years, and was from the Bay Area, where I had lived for seven years. After reading this memoir, I feel like I know him on a deeper level.

Here are a few things I gleaned about him: He opened himself up entirely as part of his healing journey. He is an introspective extrovert, always looking for spiritual lessons and opportunities for growth. He loves humankind and desires to help others struggling with similar mental, emotional, and spiritual issues. He's brave beyond measure. He may not have been able to articulate it as a child, but I believe he knew his divine "Truth" at a young age, as he does today.

June and Ward Cleaver are a Hollywood fantasy. Many of us experienced abuse, trauma, and dysfunction while growing up. Most of us lived through spankings, mean and unkind words, criticality, favoritism, perfectionism, control issues, and neglect or abandonment. The alcoholic parent who manifests chaos is not uncommon—I've heard countless emotionally-ravaging stories from friends in alcohol recovery meetings. But how many of us can say we experienced the chaos, unpredictability, and sheer terror generated by a parent who is mentally ill? Not as many of us. In this drama we call life, there are many victims and survivors, but not as many "overcomers." To paraphrase Rev. Patrick, *"It's not so much about the cards we are dealt, but how we play them."*

From childhood through adulthood, I was always told that I was too sensitive, like that was a bad thing. Deep down, I knew it wasn't. Today we see it as being in touch with our intuition or empathy. Many more people are calling themselves "empaths" in the 21st century. This state of mind is rare in a world dominated by left-brained, logical thinkers. The practice of "inner knowing" worked well for the Little Man. He used it to observe and understand others, appease unruly and mentally unstable behavior, calm a troubled or fearful mind, escape danger, and above all, protect his family. The Little Man was not a victim but a champion.

However, what impressed me the most about the Little Man was his desire for a "normal" life despite the chaos. It wasn't just a desire but an insistence. Despite my tears for this brave little kid, I cheered the Little Man on during the fateful Christmas incident you'll read about. There were several incidents like this throughout the book. I kept asking myself, "How could this young boy *survive* all this trauma and not just persevere, but *thrive*?" The answer, I believe, lies in something Greater, something Divine *within* the boy who quickly became the Little Man.

As an adult, Rev. Patrick gained a greater perspective on his healing journey. He learned the language, meaning, and techniques of deep emotional healing. Regarding his "inner child work," he writes, "*I use the technique of reframing, reclaiming, and renaming the traumatic events that took place in my childhood. As I look at the event with new eyes and a new perspective, healing takes place.*"

I look forward to his next book. I'm hoping he'll expand on these techniques in a chapter or two to help us even more. Healing isn't just an academic exercise for Rev. Patrick—he lived through the trauma, and came out the other end with love and forgiveness in his heart.

At the outset of this book, Rev. Patrick writes, *"It is my hope that others who have suffered or who are continuing to suffer the pain and shame of mental illness within themselves, or someone in their lives, will know they are not alone. I trust they will be inspired to come forward and get the help they need to heal."* I hope for this, too. In fact, I'll go out on a limb and affirm it.

I know this is the Divine Truth for those who suffer pain, shame, guilt, or fear in silence. This book helps many. Right here, right now.

Well done, R.P. Well done.

MARK REED
AUTHOR/TEACHER/PRAY-ER
JUNE 2023

Introduction

"There are scared children still left inside us, existing beneath our skin, that deserve to be held, to be given something soft to hold onto."

- KALEENA MADRUGA

As I sit at my computer starting to write this book about myself, I've placed on my desk a snapshot of me at six weeks old along with a clay handprint I made in kindergarten. As I continue to make sense of everything I am writing, I feel I was a special little boy who came to earth to learn, to grow, and to make a difference. This intuitive thought allows me to understand how I survived the chaos of my childhood and to thrive as the man I am today.

My intuitive self has always told me I have made several attempts to get here, and it was never easy to find the right parents. I have always imagined I've been through many failed attempts and mishaps to actually be born on May 2, 1958 in Heidelberg, Germany. There is something within me that has always felt I was a prince who might have been born into the wrong family. However, I know there are no mistakes. There is a purpose behind every part of our lives. It is not a random Universe. I believe in a plan, not to be mistaken as destiny, but a choice to be where we are at just the right time.

Many times, I have asked myself why I am writing this book. It must hold a purpose beyond just telling all the stories of my dysfunctional family and terrifying childhood growing up with a father who suffered a long list of diagnoses: extreme rage episodes, PTSD, bipolar disorder, alcoholism, and the final diagnosis, paranoid schizophrenia and extreme delusions.

So, you might ask, why not just journal my thoughts, get a lot of therapy, and move on? Well, I have journaled these thoughts throughout my life, although I didn't keep those journals. I have also had plenty of therapy. Both of these have helped me through the pain of my past, and still, there is a calling from within to publicly share my story in its raw totality.

As a child, my family taught me that we do not launder our private life in front of others, but I am sixty-five years old and I am putting away childish things. I am ready to tell the *whole truth and nothing but the truth* about the mental illness coverup called my childhood. My inner child demands it of me.

What is my inner child? My inner child is my place of pure untouched potential. I have spent a lifetime getting to know and embracing this inner child. I have listened to his unique voice and he has a story to tell. He wants to let you, the reader, know how he navigated through fear, pain, danger, and emotional terror to become not just a survivor, but a thriver; a loving, highly functional, and successful human being.

I have shared some of the darkest stories of growing up with my wife, friends, family, colleagues, spiritual mentors, therapists, and have even included them in my public talks and workshops. After I reveal the frightening experiences of my youth, there is always a similar thread of questions. Some of the most common questions asked are:

- How could your mother stay with your father?

- As a veteran of two wars, why didn't your father get the help he needed?
- Did you ever tell a grownup outside of your family what was going on?
- How did you turn out so well-adjusted after living in these circumstances?
- How did you deal with the constant fear of being hurt or even killed?
- Are you afraid that you inherited schizophrenia from your father?
- Do you consider yourself to have been abused?

Because I have finally dared to ask myself these same questions, the answers have been revealed through the writing of this book, and my healing has truly taken place on the deepest level.

And so, finally, why am I writing this book? My intention is to be totally honest, vulnerable, and transparent. By doing so, it is my hope that others who have suffered or who are continuing to suffer the pain and shame of mental illness within themselves or someone in their lives, will know they are not alone. I trust they will be inspired to come forward and get the help they need to heal.

The story appears to be focused on my father (the man I was raised by), but the truth is everyone in the family is involved and a participant. There are even times when I doubted my own sanity.

This book is not just for the person affected directly by mental illness, but also for the friend, the therapist, the doctor, the veteran, the abused woman or man, or even the passerby who notices someone on the street or at an event who seems different or deeply disturbed.

I have come to learn that mental illness appears in many forms and can be disguised in many ways. Do we all suffer from some form of mental illness? We cannot deny that many have experienced mental breakdowns throughout their lives. The NIMH (National Institute of Mental Health) states:

> "Mental illnesses are common in the United States. Nearly one in five U.S. adults live with a mental illness (51.5 million in 2019). Mental illnesses include many different conditions that vary in degree of severity, ranging from mild, to moderate, to severe."

Many times, while writing this book, I have compared myself to others who seem to have had it worse than me. What makes this story so special? There is no measuring stick for abuse and dysfunction. The measuring stick is unique and is in the heart of the abused.

Do I wish I never experienced this journey I am about to share with you? Of course, I would have liked to have been spared such terror and pain. Yet, since it cannot be erased from my history or my memory, what I know is that my strong inner child who speaks through these pages can serve as a GPS for others, guiding them from the darkness to the light.

So please, do not get clouded in feeling sorry for me or looking to blame the adults who raised me. I did not reveal my story to get your sympathy or to point blame anywhere. My purpose is to highlight my victory and not my defeat. My purpose is to bring compassionate understanding to all involved so as to pave a road for healing.

I have researched the politically correct way to address mental illness for this book. The proper term is *"living with mental illness."* The words never to be used are: *"afflicted* by mental illness," or "*suffers from mental illness*," or "*is a victim of mental illness.*" I apologize in advance if my words are not politically correct. I feel I was *afflicted by mental illness, suffered from mental illness* and was *victimized by mental illness*.

However, although I lost a childhood through this war with mental illness, I gained a gift as well. I have never forgotten that I was victimized, but I also remember I chose to not be a victim. My prayer is that we will spend less time on how to use politically correct terms about mental illness and spend more time assisting those who suffer because of it.

Fasten your seat belts; it might be a bumpy ride. The good news is (not to spoil the ending), love always wins. Thank you in advance for sharing my journey with me.

PATRICK FEREN

Every Story Has a Beginning

> *"A journey of a thousand miles begins with a single step."*
>
> *- LAO TZU*

On May 2, 1958, Catherine Engler, my mother, gave birth to her second son, me — Frank Patrick Engler. No, that is not a typo. I was not Patrick Feren when I was born nor when I was growing up. Much later, my mother let me know that when she first looked into my eyes, her only thought was to call me Patrick. It was because of the pressure to name me after a family member that she relented and named me Frank. She confessed she couldn't let go of her desire to call me Patrick, so it became my middle name.

I never liked the name Frank, and I didn't like being called Frankie either. Instinctively, even before my mother told me the story, I felt I was always Patrick. As a child I would doodle, writing over and over, *"My name is Patrick."*

Many years later, I would legally change my name to Patrick Feren, leaving behind both Frank and my last name, Engler. Feren was my mother's family name. I used the excuse for changing my name to being an actor who needed a different name, but I knew the real reason. I was doing my best to remove the memory of my past. If changing my name would do it, it was worth a try. But, as Shakespeare wrote, *"A rose by any other name would smell as sweet."*

1

In my case, "*sweet*" was not the word for the memories the name "Frank" held for me. And changing my name would not stamp those memories out.

If you were to view my birth certificate, you would see it reads, "Frank Patrick Engler born in Heidelberg, Germany." I showed up in Heidelberg because my father was stationed there. My father had a twenty-year military career, and by the time I arrived, he had already served in World War II and in the Korean War.

Through the years, my mother let me know my life's drama began before I was born. My father, Donovan Engler, was always in trouble with the army. His behavior was passed off as having a drinking problem but we would later find out he had a serious undiagnosed mental condition.

His reckless behavior caused him to be demoted several times. I also learned from my mother that the military were very protective of their men and women. When anyone would cause trouble, yes, they were demoted, but the mishap was always kept a secret. Apparently, it was the army's purpose to preserve its reputation.

I would later find out that I was one of those big secrets; a secret kept by my mother until I was the age of twenty-four. This secret was that I was not my father's biological son. As you will read, my family was made of secrets, and I learned to keep those secrets at all costs.

So, back to Donovan Engler, the only father I knew until the age of twenty-four. Unfortunately for my family, with each of his demotions came a pay decrease. I would hear my mother continually say, "*Your dad has no concept of what it is to earn a living.*" The burden fell on my mother to support us, and as a family, we struggled. I felt my mother's constant worry to make ends meet. I experienced both my mother's and father's partying life too. Perhaps partying provided relief during a pretty upsetting time in our history. According to my mother, party time was just a natural part of army life. She said my father's drunken rages were accepted in those times when things got out of hand. He wasn't unlike many of his army buddies, and they were all very forgiving of one another's blackouts and behavioral upsets. They were all in this together after all. As my mother explained it, I understood that the code of silence and protection stood as an emblem of loyalty for soldiers and their families.

As I look back on it with older eyes, I can see how drinking covered up my father's mental illness. With little understanding of mental illness at that time, drinking was the logical answer to a problem seeking a solution. I can also understand how drinking might have covered up the severe PTSD from which my father suffered, as it did so many of our military men and women. My father was not alone in the traumatic aftereffects of war. Today, this tragic story continues for so many.

My mother said my father changed drastically after the Korean War. Not only did his drinking increase, but he experienced a complete emotional shutdown, coupled with mood swings, and extreme paranoia. Also, his violent rages while drinking increased and were not easily controlled.

Most of what I have written about was gathered from conversations with my mother. I sometimes recall memories of being a small baby, but those are entirely too vague so I will not give any attention to them here.

California, Here We Come!

> *"California, Here I Come*
> *Right back where I started from*
> *Where bowers of flowers*
> *Bloom in the spring*
> *Each morning at dawning*
> *Birdies sing at everything*
> *A sun kissed miss said, "Don't be late!"*
> *That's why I can hardly wait (come on!)*
> *Open up (open up! open up!) that golden gate*
> *California, Here I Come"*
> - BUD DESYLVA, JOSEPH MEYER, AL JOLSON

We left Germany when I was nine months old to return to the United States. My father was stationed all over the States, making my older brother, Danny, and me, army brats; a name given to those of us who were birthed to military parents. I remember feeling like I was a member of a secret society. Military families had privileges and benefits. We had ID cards that gave us access to all kinds of goodies on the military base. We went to military doctors. We shopped in the Commissary and used the PX (Post Exchange). We even went to movies on the base. Medical coverage was a real bonus. Even when we didn't live on the base, that medical coverage helped us out financially.

Prior to living in Germany, my mother lived in the San Francisco Bay Area. She absolutely loved it there. She told me she vowed to my father over and over that if she ever returned to the Bay Area, she would stay there for the rest of her life. She almost kept that promise. She ended up living there for over fifty years.

Her fifty years began when my father received a new assignment in Oakland, California, and they moved to Peek-A-Boo Mobile Home Park. My mother told me she drove our trailer all by herself to Oakland from Alabama. I was too young to remember that trip nor do I remember that first trailer. Later, my mother would tell me she loved living in trailers more than anywhere else. I'm not sure why. Could it be because it was easier to leave when we were told we weren't welcome anymore?

And, that's just what happened. Not long after settling at the Peek-A-Boo Mobile Home Park, my father caused some type of trouble. The people in charge said, although we kids and my mother could stay, my father wasn't welcome. Well, we weren't going to leave Dad behind so we packed up and made our way to our next home in Richmond, California.

Years later when I was working toward a degree in criminal justice, I remember the instructor mentioning that the highest crime and murder rate per capita were in the cities of Richmond, San Pablo, and Oakland. I was about to grow up in Richmond, and then San Pablo, and my mother went to work for Ryerson Steel in Oakland/Emeryville. As you will come to learn, my early life was a crime scene in itself and this crime scene extended outside my home into my neighborhood and town.

Although my father had the opportunity to spend his whole life in the army, Oakland was his last assignment. It was at this time he retired. I was only four years old. Army retirement at that time was a couple hundred dollars a month. My mother told me later she begged my father not to retire. Her begging wasn't just because of the financial burden his retirement would cause, but because she knew it was the only thing he knew how to do. My father argued the point with her, "*I will be better, Katie, if I can just get out of this situation. I won't drink as much, and I won't act up as much.*" He would continue the argument with, "*I am unhappy because of the military and that is why I drink so much.*"

Whenever a change was demanded due to some ill behavior on my father's part, he repeated this argument over and over. My mother said she was always hopeful about his promises, but time and time again, she continued to be disappointed. Now I can see that my mother refused to see the possibility those promises held was just an illusion. As I recall, I took on that belief. However, things never got better, and I eventually lost that hope.

Upon his retirement, my father went on to do his best to live in an unfamiliar and unprotected world where his violent and drunken episodes would not be hidden, like they were with the army. We would soon find out how he would handle the freedom of not being told what to do in every moment. After he left the army, he never really held down a job. It wasn't that he wasn't talented enough. For example, he was a great carpenter and he was good at math. The problem was the bottle, compounded by a lack of confidence in himself. I would soon find out he was harboring another secret. It was why my mother always filled out his job applications. At first, I thought it was about his resistance to work, but later I would come to learn he only had a fourth-grade education. That was a real embarrassment to both him and my mother. I remember her crying about it. It probably added to her fear of his inability to hold down a job.

After leaving the Peek-A-Boo, we moved to Clinton Avenue in Richmond, California. It was a real house. I'm not sure why we didn't move to another one of my mother's beloved mobile home parks. Maybe my father made another one of those promises that he would be better if they got out of trailer park living.

Richmond was divided into two parts: the Heights and the not-so-Heights. Our house on Clinton was in the Heights. My mother said they purchased that home through my father's GI loan. They paid $13,000 for it. As of the writing of this book, it's worth at least a million, maybe more in the current upward trend in real estate.

Although the Peek-A-Boo Trailer Park is a blur, I do remember moving to Clinton Avenue. I was five years old. I remember it giving me a feeling of fun and hope. We even had our first dog. Her name was Mitty. Maybe, just maybe, Dad would be better. It was a new beginning. We were in a neighborhood where no one knew us or our history. However, my hope would soon be dashed against the stronger and monstrous rock of my father's mental illness. We would soon prove that *"wherever you go, there you are."*

In the beginning of our life on Clinton Avenue, there was a definite calm; a peace before the storm that would eventually take us over once again. Yes, we had a few glorious moments in that house. As we moved in, I remember exploring the empty space before the furniture arrived. It was huge compared to our little trailer at Peek-A-Boo. Danny and I shared a bedroom and a bunk bed with a distant view of the Golden Gate Bridge. The room was small but the view was large. I felt like I was on top of the world. Christmas time was magical. As I laid in that bunk bed, which by the way, was made by my father, I was barely able to fall asleep. I remember listening and watching for Santa.

I haven't said much about my brother, Danny, before this because he was seven years older than me. As I became more conscious of my life, I became more aware of Danny and our stormy relationship, which I will get into soon.

Back to those bunk beds. They weren't the only thing my father built. In spite of everything else, as I previously said, father was a great carpenter and he created a lot of furniture over the years. He turned our garage on Clinton into his carpentry studio. I wanted to visit him there and watch him turn wood into chairs and cabinets and dressers. It seemed magical to me. However, he never let me. "*That's my private place, Frankie,*" he'd gently chide me. I was disappointed but respected his need for privacy while he was working. I would eventually find out that his carpentry studio was also his secret bar. He could drink there and not get caught by my mother. I remember sneaking in and seeing those empty and half-filled bottles. I never told my mother what I found. I had a need to protect all of my family. Yes, my ability to keep secrets was one of my modes of protection for all of us. Hiding and protecting was built into my DNA.

Mom called me her "*Little Man,*" and I was just that. When my father could not be the man of the house, which was most of the time, I stepped in to do what I had to do to keep everyone safe, especially my mother. She eventually found out about my father's secret bar without my help. She didn't do anything about it. Maybe my father's spectacular carpentry skills made up for his other deficiencies. As I look back, it doesn't make sense. Maybe, we humans purposefully overlook the things closest to us until we are pushed into a corner and have no choice. My family's corners were very deep and our secrets stayed hidden there for many years.

One of the most amazing things my father built was a deck. My mother loved sports and she'd sit out on the deck on weekends, drinking a cold beer, listening to the San Francisco Giants baseball games or the San Francisco 49er football games on her transistor radio. How did she acquire this alone time within the chaos? Well, Dad hated sports. Danny shared my mother's love for sports, but he was too busy playing them to sit on that deck with her. I could tell my mother didn't mind those Saturday afternoons by herself. I'd sometimes peek at her out there. I was young but could sense it was a time of peace for her. Seeing my mother relaxed brought peace to me. We were that connected.

I practiced my role as Little Man at times like that. The Little Man became what I called the "*appeaser*." I knew how to appease my father and my mother knew that I did. She probably didn't want to be interrupted from those peaceful moments on the deck. Sometimes, my father would scream out drunk from the bedroom. I remember my mother saying, "*Go appease your father, Frankie.*" I knew exactly how to do that but I will get into that story later. I do not believe my mother knew she was sending me into what would become the beginning of my rite of passage at seven years old.

Building a Life in Crisis on Clinton Avenue

"Forgiveness says you are given another chance to make a new beginning."

- DESMOND TUTU

There were no kids my age in the Clinton Avenue neighborhood except Jill. She had three older sisters and their father worked for a big oil company. He must have had an important position because they even had a maid who took care of the kids and cleaned the house. I remember playing at her house. I'd be asked to leave around dinner time. Jill told me she and her sisters had to eat before her father came home. She explained that when her father arrived, her mother had a fancy candlelit dinner and wine waiting for him. I didn't understand a mealtime like this. My life was so different.

My mother strove to make our dinners normal. She was a good cook and we were well-nourished. Every night, we ate at the same time — 6 o'clock. Although many of our dinners ended with some sort of drama caused by my father, my mother was persistent. Dishes might have been thrown against a wall or my father might have been drunk, his face in the mash potatoes. We might have had to run for our lives into the night, but dinnertime went on every night on schedule.

A boy my age moved into the neighborhood. His name was Billy and he had a learning disability which made him seem much younger than me. It made him seem less intelligent too. In those days, we didn't know all the terms for learning disabilities that we have today. We just called him, "*slow*." My need to protect the weak soon found me protecting Billy. I helped him with his homework and made sure no one made fun of him.

I also remember spending a lot of time alone at home and I didn't mind it. I had a great imagination and played make-believe games. I had a strong habit of spending a lot of time redecorating and rearranging my room. I didn't know it at the time, but I was told by a therapist that my constant need to rearrange the furniture in my bedroom was my way of being in charge of my life. I think that was true as I felt very out of control in so many ways. Unconsciously, I was learning how to maneuver my way through a very confusing environment.

Even at this early age, my intuition was definitely heightened. I believe that this heightened awareness and my power of observation allowed me to survive as a child living in a dysfunctional and dangerous family setting. The family danger extended to my father's family also. His parents lived in Nebraska so we rarely saw them. However, the few times we did visit them were scary times for me. I was afraid to be alone with my grandpa. I would beg my mother not to leave me with him. I had no outward reason for being afraid, but I knew something wasn't right with him.

Psychology professionals might say this intuition was birthed out of the need to survive, but I feel I came here with it. I would later find out that my hunch was true. Yes, there is scientific evidence that we receive signals from our mother in the womb. These signals build our personality in order to help us adjust and cope in the environment into which we are born.

As I wrote before, I was later to find out my father, Donovan Engler, was not my biological father. Mom also let me know that this was the secret that pressured her to call me Frank instead of Patrick. She told me she often prayed to God that I might look different than my biological father. She prayed that I wouldn't have his dimples and that my hair would be straight. Is it possible that I rearranged my gene expression in the womb along with building my strong intuition and coping skills? Here is some scientific research from cellular biologist and author, Dr. Bruce Lipton.

> "We used to think that only nutrition was provided by the mother to a developing child. The story was genes control the development; the mother just provides nutrition. We now know, of course, that there's more than just nutrition in blood. Blood contains information about emotions and regulatory hormones and the growth factors that control the mother's life in the world in which she's living. All this information passes into the placenta along with nutrition. If the mother is happy, the fetus is happy because the same chemistry of emotions that affect the mother's system are crossing into the fetus. If the mother is scared or stressed, the same stress hormones cross and adjust the fetus. What we're recognizing is that through a concept called epigenetics, the environmental information is used to select and modify the genetic program of the fetus so it will conform to the environment in which

it's going to grow, thus enhancing the survival of the child. If parents are totally unaware, this creates a great problem — they don't know that their attitudes and responses to their experiences are being passed on to their child."

- BRUCE LIPTON NEWSLETTER, NOVEMBER 21, 2014

My mother was most definitely unaware of what her fears and doubts might have been communicating to me. I even go beyond this scientific theory. I also believe we have a prenatal spiritual contract which gives us the exact family we require in order to spiritually evolve. This might seem simply speculative on my part, but I do strongly believe in the continuity of life and our continuous evolution as a species. Although this helps me to explain my ability to cope and maneuver my way through the life-threatening situations of my childhood, at the time, I simply did what I felt I needed to do.

***

As a child, I went to Woodrow Wilson Elementary School. With no family in the area and my mother's need to work, she had to hire a babysitter to take care of us after school. Our babysitter wasn't a relative, but we called her Nana. I met my best friend, Bruce Wilson, at Nana's. His mother was like mine. She was the main provider and she worked all day. However, she was divorced. I was curious about this thing called divorce and wondered if my mother ever thought about divorcing my father. She said she stayed with my father for security but he was always out of a job. I knew she could support us, just like Bruce's mother, but it wasn't a subject I talked about with her until much later.

Even though my mother paid Nana for taking care of us, Nana was like family. She even knew the secret about my father. She never told anyone, maybe because she had plenty of secrets of her own. Her husband died by suicide, using a gun to end his life. Her daughter, Kelly, lived with extreme depression and prescription and alcoholism addiction. Kelly died by suicide by jumping off the Golden Gate Bridge. Her son Sam died by suicide by leaping from the San Rafael Bridge.

Yes, Nana had an overabundance of tragedies. I think those tragedies made her older than her years because she always appeared really old to me. However, I always looked at Nana as a model of strength, just like my own mother. I loved my Nana. Nana did a lot for me that my mother couldn't do because of her work schedule. I don't remember feeling bad that Nana would be the one to take me to things like my kindergarten orientation and other daytime school activities. I knew that my mother had to work. She made that clear to me.

There was a big tree at Nana's house that holds a lot of memories for me. The kids at Nana's would climb to the top and then scream down to me to come up. I just couldn't do it. You see, my mother always instructed me not to get hurt. *"If you get hurt, Frankie, I'll have to miss work. I can't do that. We need the money because your dad doesn't have a job right now. Mom needs her Little Man to stay safe."* I understood my responsibility as the Little Man in regards to not getting hurt. Her calling me the Little Man was my badge of courage. I never climbed that tree, not because I was afraid, but because I didn't want to take the chance of being responsible for my mother losing even a day at work, or worse yet, losing her job. That was the least this Little Man could do.

Later in life, I went back to Nana's to visit. I thought I'd climb that tree but the tree had been cut down. I sat on the stump with a lump of regret in my heart for never having climbed it. However, the Little Man in me knew that the decision not to climb that tree was yet another decision along with a lifetime of others to take care of my mother and the family.

Whenever my father was in a drunken rage, Nana's house was our safe place. While he slept it off at home, she welcomed us many times in the middle of the night, letting us sleep on the couch and on her floor. We were like those kids who had to run to shelters. We didn't run to shelters because those nights of violence and alcohol were kept a secret. No one knew and we were sworn to secrecy. Our life was so normal during the day that no one would have suspected what went on at night. I always give great gratitude for Nana who made me feel safe in spite of the violence that raged around me.

Even now, as a man, I am also grateful that Nana never told our secret. You might ask, "Why?" If she had, I might have been taken away from my mother, and even beyond that, as strange as it sounds, I wouldn't want to change any part of my history. Why? Because changing any part of one's history changes the present. I wouldn't be who I am today without my past. This might not be understandable to some who read this book, who might have experienced their own turbulent past. However, for me, through the process of reframing, reclaiming, and renaming the events and experiences of my past, I have been able, and continue to, practice forgiveness. This practice allows me to let go of the emotions that keep me from living in the glorious present moment. I will explain this more fully at the end of my story.

Danny

"We must live together as brothers or perish together as fools."

- MARTIN LUTHER KING, JR.

As a child, I always seemed to find strength in women. There certainly weren't any men to look up to at my house. However, the men in my house, which included my father and my older brother Danny, thought I should look up to them. It was their job to teach me, as they put it, "*to man up.*" They let me know they were experts on what women really wanted. Drinking a lot was also a prerequisite to being a man.

I would spend my whole life looking for a male role model and I took many roads to find one. When I decided to enter therapy, I sought out a woman therapist. At our first session, she noted how easy it was for me to talk to her. She asked if it was always easy for me to talk to women. I pondered her question for a moment and replied in the positive. She let me know that I would make better progress in my healing with a male therapist and referred me to one she knew and trusted. I will always thank her for that because it was my male therapist who helped me cross the bridge to knowing men as good and trustworthy.

As the years unfolded, it became clear to me that my brother wished I'd never been born. He tried to hurt me on many occasions. I feel that he literally hated me. Was it because my birth forced him to give up his only-child status or was it more than that? I could justify the reasons for his behavior toward me, but much is left to speculation as we never discussed it.

Danny was a jock, good at sports and popular with his friends. One thing I remember about Danny was his high school blue jean binder that all his friends would write on. I thought that was the coolest thing in the world. I am aware there is a cliché that older siblings do not want to be around their younger siblings, but Danny's disdain for me was so apparent, his friends even asked him why he was so mean to me. "*Let him tag along with us. It's okay,*" they'd encourage him.

Danny never budged in his feelings toward me. He kept me away from his life. His way of bonding with our father was to put me down and make fun of me. He loved being part of what my father thought was just fun and games – finding ways to tease Frankie. Whenever we'd watch TV together and there was a commercial for little girl's toys or dolls, Danny and Dad would both chime in, "*Wouldn't Frankie love that little doll?*"

"*Sissy*" was their name for me. I remember begging them, "*Stop it!*" I'd scream. "*Stop calling me that!*" but they never did. Where was my mother? If she was there, she'd intervene but that only made things worse. Later, they'd ridicule me and call me a sissy who needed defending. As we know, kids that are bullied seldom tell anyone about their experiences for the same reasons. I was no different.

Danny saw our father's cruel side too. My father was quite the chameleon, and when he was drunk, he would sometimes turn on Danny. When Dad scorned him, Danny was good at hiding his feelings. Later, that would do him more harm as he never got help with processing his childhood. After many years of drug abuse, alcohol, and violence, his life would end early.

At some fork in the road, I went one way and he went the other. I wonder how two people who grow up in the same environment turn out so differently, but I've come to realize that everyone is on their own journey. It's not about the cards we are dealt; it is about the kind of hands we play with those cards.

Before Danny would turn his anger inward, he continued to take it out on me. That was the case on this particular night. My mother never trusted my father to watch me because he might get drunk. However, on rare occasions when she had to leave me with him, she gave Danny the responsibility of taking care of me. I'm not sure why she thought Danny was a good babysitter for me because later she would tell me she was aware of his volatile behavior. I think she was in some kind of denial about him. I might be her Little Man, but Danny was her pride and joy. Desperate to keep working to support us, I'm sure this compounded her decision to let him take care of me.

On one particular night, we were watching TV when one of those doll commercials came on. Without my mother present, the teasing got pretty bad. I got up to go to the bedroom to try to get away, but Dad and Danny continued to taunt me, "*Oh, do you have to go to the bedroom to play with your dolls, little girl?*" Dad tormented me.

Danny joined in, "*He can't take us calling him a girl, Dad. He's such a sissy.*"

As I tried to get away, Dad grabbed me. "*Let me go!*" I screamed.

"*We are just playing with you. Don't be such a baby girl,*" Danny laughed.

They seemed to be having more than a good time teasing me this time, and I was scared. My father play-wrestled me to the ground, pinning me there while Danny cheered him on. I screamed and wiggled to get away. Danny just laughed and yelled, "*Get him, Dad!*" I was raging with hurt because my brother was siding with a man who seriously threatened both of us on numerous occasions. How could I not get it? Danny hated me. "*I'm gonna tell Mom, and you're both going to be in big trouble,*" I yelped. I shouldn't have said that because it just egged them on and they continued to pin me down and laugh.

"*Mom ain't here to protect you now, is she? I've got you now. Your mine, little girl.*" Dad laughed hysterically.

I started crying and Danny continued laughing, "*Aw, sissy, we're just having fun. Why are you such a sissy?*"

My father started rubbing is stubbly beard on me from one side of my face to the other. It was like sandpaper to my skin. It hurt and I was screaming, but he just kept rubbing that stubble on my face and making this horrible shrieking noise, "*Ehhhhhhhh!*"

As I look back on that night, I liken it to the brutal sex scene in the film, Deliverance, when the backwoods redneck was chasing the guy, treating him like a pig, and yelling, "*Sooey Sooey!*"

This was this scene without the sex, but with as much brutality. To this day, I cannot watch that film.

I felt trapped and humiliated. My face was sore and burning from Dad's beard. "*Please stop!*" I cried and begged. They didn't relent. Instead, Dad picked me up by the feet like a piece of meat dangling on a rope and ran to the bathroom. He then began to dunk my head in the toilet. *"Let's just wash your hair. Get that sissy out of you,"* he laughed in delirium.

I wiggled and struggled as he continued to pull me in and out of the toilet while my brother flushed it. As I write this, I can still hear the sound of the handle and that whooshing sound of water as Danny flushed it over and over. I can still hear the sound of their laughing and jeering torments while I screamed and cried. Then, all of a sudden, they just let me go and dumped me on the bathroom floor. As if nothing had happened and without a word, they left me there and went back to watching TV.

I now acknowledge that what happened to me was a form of rape. I was held down against my will, laughed at, made fun of, hurt physically, verbally abused, and physically humiliated. After their fun was over, I had to put myself emotionally and physically back together. It was a big job for a six-year-old. Danny and Dad's message was: This is just how guys have fun. There is no harm intended. As I made my way to my bedroom to clean up, Dad called back to me, *"And don't tell Mommy, sissy!"*

"Yeah, sissy!" repeated Danny.

"Don't tell Mommy!" and *"Yeah, sissy!"* is all I had to take into my bedroom. As I reflected on what had just happened to me, I remember that telling my mother was the first thing I wanted to do. When she walked through that door, I wanted to run to her and let her know what they had done to me.

Alone in my bedroom, I stared out the window at the big city of San Francisco in the distance all lit up like the Emerald City in *The Wizard of Oz*. I pictured myself finding that yellow brick road that would take me there with my dog, Mitty, my own Toto. But Mitty was in the living room with

Dad and Danny and I was trapped with nowhere to go. I was so angry and hurt. I went to pull out my secret diary to write my feelings down but I was afraid Danny might come in and make fun of me for having a diary. *"Only girls have diaries,"* he'd taunted me before.

Even though it had a key, he might even rip it from my hands before I could lock it and read all of my feelings out loud. No! I decided writing my feelings down was too dangerous. I was very confused and wondered if what they said about me was really true? Was I a sissy? I was always called sensitive by my mother and others. My mother would say, *"Don't be so sensitive!"* It felt more like something bad rather than a compliment. Was I too sensitive? Was I not boy enough? Was this why this happened to me? Was it okay to hurt girls like this? Even at my young age, I wondered why men thought it was okay to treat girls or women so terribly.

"But, I am not a girl! I am a boy!" I told myself. Just because I didn't like sports didn't make me a girl. I didn't like them because I wasn't good at them. When we played games at school, the captains avoided me. I was always last to be picked. It wasn't until much later that it dawned on me that the captains didn't want me on their team because they wanted to win. It had nothing to do with them not liking me or thinking I was a sissy.

Danny was the sports jock in our home. I accepted that, even though it made him a favorite in my mother's eyes. On the other hand, my father hated sports. Now that was really confusing, since my dad thought he was a real man.

As I sat in my room, thinking all these thoughts and wanting my mother to come home so I could feel protected from Danny and Dad, I wondered if I could possibly be blaming myself in some strange way for this happening to me. Beneath the sound of the blaring TV in the living room, I could hear them talking and laughing. It might have been at my expense, but Danny had gotten a moment to have our father all to himself. I imagined he was savoring the moment. However, I knew it was just a matter of time before my father would be insulting Danny and screaming, "*You're not my son!*" A part of me couldn't wait for that moment to come.

My mother finally returned home and I ran to the door to greet her. Danny and Dad looked at me in a way that made me feel they might actually be afraid I would say something to expose them and this awful night. "*How did everything go tonight?*" Mom asked. I looked at Danny and Dad, and then looked at my mother. I paused, feeling a strange sense of power. I couldn't do it. I knew if I did tell, it would end up worse for me at some other time. "*Everything was fine, Mom,*" I said quietly and simply.

These were my male role models. However, a role model can also teach you what you do not want to be like. I believe you can choose to not repeat the patterns of your dysfunctional upbringing. I definitely did not want to be like my father or my brother. I knew it was wrong to make someone suffer. I knew I would take a different path. I wouldn't become that kind of man.

How did I have this discernment at such an early age? That is a question I often contemplate. I know I wasn't a saint. I made plenty of my own mistakes in my social and intimate relationships. However, I would not become a bully, an abuser, or purposefully take another's free will away. Instead, time and time again, I would seek out drama in my relationships and become the bullied one, until I learned to let go of the patterns of recreating drama in my life.

I am not sure if I ever did tell my mother about that night.

It is hard to imagine that I didn't tell her since throughout our relationship, I told her everything. I'm also not sure my mother knew until much later how Danny treated me. Again, maybe she was just in denial. Danny was the star of the family in my mother's eyes. Along with being the star athlete, he was always on the Dean's list. He was constantly receiving an award for something and he often appeared in our local newspaper. My mother bragged about him all the time. All my brother's accolades and achievements were displayed under the glass of her desk at work. People who knew us thought my mother had only one child. She let me know later that people at her work would ask, *"Don't you have another child?"*

Although Danny seemed to be her favorite, I knew my mother loved me. I had something else that she prized. I protected the family secret. It didn't bring me a claim to fame and public notoriety, but being my mother's Little Man, confidant, and protector had its own quiet reward that superseded it all. In my little mind, I felt big and strong and special because of it. Much later, my mother would tell me that she never forgave herself for leaving me in Danny's care. She would tell me about the time she left him to babysit me when I was one year old, only to come home and find me at the top of a staircase without a sign of Danny anywhere. Did he put me there? I'll never know.

***

As Danny grew older, he was diagnosed as bipolar. He became addicted to heroin, wandered the country living under freeways, and conned his way through life. He would meet a family and get in their good graces, con them in some way and then escape, only to wander again.

On one occasion, I remember getting a call from the FBI. They came to the house looking for my brother because they thought we were hiding him. He had committed a federal crime by stealing a car and taking it over the border. They had caught him but lost him at a truck stop when he conned them into letting him go to the restroom without his handcuffs. Yes, he was a charmer with a silver tongue. It wasn't the first time he had escaped the FBI.

I never really understood why Danny disliked me and was so jealous of me when he was my mother's obvious favorite. The bigger question was: Why wasn't I jealous of Danny? In spite of it all, I looked up to him. I seemed to disregard all the fear and brutality he afflicted on me and my mother. Instead, I tried to see the good in him. I remember one time trying to encourage him to write a book about all his travels. I even drove to Napa to meet him at his request. He said he wanted to take my headshot to someone he knew on the show, *Falcon Crest*. I trusted he had changed. I felt an inner excitement when he said he wanted to try to have a relationship with me. Then, in the next breath, he asked me for $100. In that moment, I realized I was just one of his cons.

Danny finally released his heroin addiction but alcohol remained his demon. My mother always dreaded the phone call that she must have intuitively felt she would someday receive. Danny was forty-two years old when that call finally came. He had been hit by a car. The hospital official informed my mother he was on life support and was probably not going to make it. I traveled with her to the hospital where we made the decision to let Danny go. I will never forget how his death affected my mother. For quite some time, I thought she wouldn't make it. She lost all emotion and vibrancy for life.

I'm Not Stupid!

"It is done unto you as you believe."
- MATHEW 9:29

"Hey, Freckle Face Strawberry! Where'd you get such a strawberry face? Did you drink some Kool-Aid?"

That's what they called me in public grade school — *Freckle Face Strawberry* — after a character in the Kool-Aid commercials. Kool-Aid was a sugar drink of our time. I think it's still around but probably not as popular during these days of health food and fads. I've kept that red face to this day, and I will say that I still have to work on not getting triggered when someone asks me if I am sunburned or have problems with my blood pressure. Just recently, during one of my runs on a local bike path here on Kaua`i, someone, thinking he was funny, got a little cruel about it.

He screamed out to me, *"I feel like having a lobster, don't you?"*

Of course, I knew he was referring to my red face which was extra red due to the exertion of running. I tried to brush it off, making some joke, but I will admit I felt the shame. I'm not sure what made this person feel like he could make fun of me in this way. That didn't matter as much as what I chose to do in that moment. I didn't just continue running and ignoring the shame I felt. Instead, I pulled that inner child out and gave him the comfort and listening to that he needed. I had to let my little boy know that it was okay to feel hurt. He let me know he was angry.

"*What would make you feel better?*" I asked.

That part of myself whispered, "*I want to cut off my face!*"

Thinking I could bring some humor to it, I said, "*That wouldn't work because no one would recognize you.*"

My little boy didn't go for the joke. He was still angry and I had to just let that be, realizing I still had work to do in this area. Just because we think we've released those triggers from childhood doesn't necessarily make it so. Until you release the emotion attached to the trigger, it still lingers in the subconscious. It's about not being afraid to bring it to your conscious mind that allows us to begin the work of releasing past trauma. As you can see from this example, I am still working on it.

So, back to my childhood. Between name-calling, bullying, and being stressed and fearful about my home life, I was a defensive kid. I was afraid of fighting, but I was in fights all the time. I would come home with ripped clothes. This upset my mother, not so much for fear that I'd been hurt, but because of the minimal clothing budget she had for us.

My first-grade teacher, Mrs. Lee, was the mean, scary kind you see in movies. She was so strict that we were even afraid to ask to go to the bathroom. I remember one little girl wetting herself rather than raise her hand. There were always puddles under her seat. Mrs. Lee belittled her and everyone in the class made fun of her. I felt such pain for the girl and wanted to protect her but I remained silent. I might confront my father but I couldn't confront Mrs. Lee. She had a whole school on her team. I knew my limits. Mrs. Lee didn't think very highly of me either. I was a shy child and she mistook that for lack of intelligence. At a parent-teacher conference, with me present, Mrs. Lee informed my mother I would never be smart enough to go on to higher education.

My mother, for the most part, never let people talk about us without speaking up. You couldn't be married to my father and not have some defense skills. However, for some reason, she didn't speak up to Mrs. Lee that day. Later, she told me she always regretted not telling Mrs. Lee off. She didn't tell me why she didn't. I often wonder if it was because, at the time, she believed Mrs. Lee's evaluation of my intelligence. A part of me believed Mrs. Lee too. It took me many years to claim my intelligence and ability to succeed in school. Eventually, I would have other mentors along the way to drown out Mrs. Lee's voice.

I now know that you have to believe in yourself. After many years of self-help, I came to that understanding. I would finally finish college at age fifty-four and would be the graduation speaker representing my class. Although it was difficult and expensive to finish that college education, I knew it was part of my healing.

Returning to my elementary school experience, I would get these incredible stomach aches during school hours. Those stomach aches got me out of school and away from Mrs. Lee. My mother couldn't come get me because she was working. Instead, Nana would get someone to watch her daycare so she could come to get me. Nana didn't have a car and it was a long walk, but like I said before, Nana was like family to us. My mother wasn't happy about all this, and after too many of these episodes, she finally realized I wasn't made for public school. She decided to see if she could enroll me at St. David's Catholic School. In order to do this, I would have to take a test. Taking tests was my worst fear because it might disclose my "unintelligence." Mrs. Lee found out I was trying to get into parochial school and she let me know

I'd never make it there. *"You're just not intelligent, Frankie."*

I can still recall the Saturday I took the test to get into Saint David's. I was terrified. I had a nervous stomach all day. I remembered feeling stupid as I bought into Mrs. Lee's assessment of my intellect. I never thought I would pass that test. However, I believe there was a stronger part of me that took the exam. It was that part of me that wanted to prove Mrs. Lee wrong and finally get away from her. I took it early in the morning. The very solemn nun in charge said she would be calling my mother with results that same evening. I was, of course, nervous all day. I wouldn't leave the house and I spent a lot of time eyeing the phone on the kitchen wall. When it finally rang and my mother answered, I was standing right by her, holding my breath. I wanted to run to my room, but my feet were glued to the floor as I listened to my mother's response. All she said was, *"Yes, I understand. Yes, thank you very much."*

She hung up and then turned to me with a big smile. Yes, I was in! It was that simple. Goodbye forever, Mrs. Lee! I'm not sure if my excitement was about going to Catholic school or if I just was relieved and happy that I wasn't stupid. After all, how could I be stupid if I got into Saint David's?

Wherever You Are, There You Are

"Your miracles are an inside job. Go there to create the magic that you seek in your life."
- WAYNE W. DYER

Transferring to Catholic school felt like the beginning of a whole new life for me. It felt so new and different. Would it be a new beginning at home too? I hoped so. However, my hope quickly disintegrated into despair. Things were still horrible at home. My father didn't change when we moved to Clinton Avenue and my attendance at St. David's didn't help or change him either. In fact, he seemed to be getting worse. He would have these nervous fits that always seem to come out of nowhere. I would often catch him talking to someone who wasn't there. Sometimes he would go into a rage and start screaming in what sounded like Chinese. I don't think it was really Chinese, but how was I to know?

He'd suddenly scream, *"Get down. They're here!"*

If we didn't move quickly enough, he would get extremely angry. *"Duck, Duck!"* He would then begin screaming in another language.

My father never seemed to get along with the neighbors and he still blamed them for his life not working. In his paranoia, he was sure the neighbors had it out for him. He'd tell us how they were plotting to kill him. *"I'd better get to them first!"* he'd scream.

Sometimes, as a neighbor would walk down the street, he'd shout out, *"There is that son-of-a-bitch. You cocksucker, I see you, you bastard. You can't hide from me. Your wife is a whore and you know it."*

Then he'd turn to me and say, *"You see the way he is looking at the house?"*

He'd run out to the front yard with signs he'd made, saying a variety of not-so-nice things. My mother or I would somehow coax him back into the house. I was so embarrassed.

Our backdrop was the 1960s so there was a lot going on in those days to activate my father's fears and paranoia. Now we know his unattended and severe PTSD was at the root of it all, but at the time, we continued to blame it all on his drinking. He would put his hand-written signs outside the windows of our home and in the back window of his car, saying, *"STAY AWAY FROM ME!"* and *"I SEE YOU!"* and *"I SEE YOU, BLACK PANTHERS!"*

He would even use the "N" word on his signs. I wondered how my mother could live with a man who wore his rage on his sleeve, while at the same time knowing that the neighbors had to hear everything. She most definitely did care what the neighbors thought. It was another contradiction in her I still do not understand to this day.

My father was still in constant need of employment. He'd either quit or get fired after drinking on the job. He had several security jobs watching properties that were under construction. He usually worked graveyard shifts. One of the sites even gave him a gun because he had been in the army. That really made me nervous.

My mother was desperate for my father to keep his job so he could help with the finances, so his job became our job as well. I use the word "*our*" to let you know that I was my mother's partner in this effort. It came with the near impossible mission to keep him sober. In fact, it was a hopeless effort and a battle we never won. "*Get in the car, Frankie! We have to check on your dad!*" she'd command me desperately on many nights. Into the car, we'd go. She didn't seem to care that it was the middle of the night. I think she thought if we checked on him, we could protect him from getting caught if he was misbehaving or drunk. On one of our particular check-up times, we found him passed out drunk in the car with a bottle of liquor on his lap. We couldn't save him. That job ended shortly after that.

When he landed the job at Jacuzzi Pumps, my mother and I were excited. It was a union job and an opportunity to make some real money. At Jacuzzi Pumps, he seemed to be doing well. He was drinking less, but his people skills were never very good. His lack of education, his mental instability, and a long list of self-esteem issues always arose on the job. We just waited and hoped those issues wouldn't show up at this one. "*Please, God!*" I prayed, "*Let this be the job that saves our family!*"

My father's paydays were stressful days for my mother and me. So much so that she would work through her lunch hour so she could get off early to meet him before he had time to cash his check and head to the Silver Dollar Bar. Many times, she did not make it. He'd come home drunk and without a penny after buying everyone at the bar drinks. How he ever got home in that state, I don't know. Sometimes, he would come home with strangers he'd met at those bars. They were all in that partying and drunken state and it was hard to remove them from the house. There were times when they stole from us. It was a nerve-racking and frightening time for all of us.

My mother's stress would become my stress, especially when I witnessed her disappointment, disgust, anger, hurt, and defeat. Oh, believe me, she wasn't passive about him spending his paycheck before contributing to the household. I witnessed their battles. She would scream and shout many things to this man who had no concept of responsibility. I wanted to help but the Little Man was powerless to keep her calm or to make my father a better provider.

My father eventually fell off a forklift at Jacuzzi Pumps and got an insurance settlement. Although this windfall would allow us to breathe financially for a bit, my father was getting worse. Paying bills continued to be a struggle for us. I don't know how many times I watched my mother crying when opening the phone bill to see it was over $100. That was a lot of money back in those days. How did we rack up those bills? My father had found himself another job. It was making long distance calls to the FBI in Washington, D.C., telling them the Black Panthers were after him. I would hate it when I'd see the phone bill arrive in the mail. I'd hold my breath, afraid that those FBI calls would be on those bills. If they were, I was guaranteed a screaming match between my parents. I stood helplessly as I witnessed these tirades.

"How am I going to pay these bills?" Mom would cry in rage. "Why, Don? Why are you doing this to me? I beg you to stop! I can't afford to pay them."

In my father's mind he was doing good to let the FBI know he was on to the bad guys, those Black Panthers. He let my mother know that. The fights continued with no solution. When he thought the FBI was turning on him, he would get even more anxious and wild. There were times I'd come home from school to find him on the phone with the FBI. I would sneak up behind him and hang up the phone to save another expensive charge on the bill. Of course, he would go into a rage at my interference and I often had to run for my life. I didn't mind. The Little Man was saving his family from a financial disaster. I felt so responsible. I often told myself I couldn't wait until I was old enough to work so I could help my mother with the finances.

The phone bill nightmare took me and my mother to the phone company close to midnight on the due date. I remember jumping out of the car and slipping the bill into the night slot so it was credited the day it was due, but not cashed until the next day. In time, my mother found a way to get the phone company to block the FBI's number. Those days of watching her trying to balance an entire family made me sad for all of us. I tried my best to hold her and my whole family up, even if only by sheer mental will. I hoped things would get better but we were a family held hostage. It would be a long time and many nightmarish episodes of insanity before my father would get a proper diagnosis.

In spite of all this, my mother continued to drink with my father, which I didn't understand. I never thought of her as an alcoholic because she only drank on the weekends. I remember hearing the parties at our next-door neighbor's house with lots of cowboy music and loud talking. She was over there drinking with my father but she knew when to stop. Maybe it was because she knew she needed to stay sober to protect us from his drunken rages.

And God Sacrificed His Only Son

> *"O my Father, if it be possible, let this cup pass from me."*
>
> - JESUS

I'm no longer a practicing Catholic, and when asked about my former religion, I always answer, "*I am not a recovering Catholic; I am a discovering Catholic.*" What does this mean? Well, I discovered what worked for me and left behind what did not. I have no ill will in regards to the religion of my childhood. I am grateful for my Catholic roots and I truly believe that those roots gave me many of the coping mechanisms that assisted me in dealing with the extreme dysfunction of my family.

As Catholics, we weren't allowed to go to God directly with our problems, so instead, I became friends with Mother Mary and the different saints and begged them to take my prayers to God. I trusted these invisible forces. I would say my belief in their existence gave me a bit of peace during my father's rages. The mystical belief in the invisible taught in all my early morning religion classes allowed me to believe in something bigger than my horrendous home life. I believed in the power of prayer even though I saw no evidence of its answers in my life.

As a little boy, I made a lot of promises to God. I remember promising God I would become a priest if He would keep my mother from being hurt or dying. I was very willing to offer up my life for the protection of my family. To tell you the truth, being a priest didn't seem like a sacrifice to me because at the time I loved my religion. My religious education taught me that I had to suffer in order to prove my love to God. It was the price I had to pay for Adam and Eve's sin. I didn't really understand why a loving God would make us suffer, but I think in my little head, it justified the suffering we went through in our house. Since we definitely suffered at the hands of my father, it seemed logical there must be an ounce of truth to suffering being part of God's plan.

I looked for ways of proving my love for God, hoping it would relieve the suffering of the world. One night, I remember taking all the sheets, blankets, and pillows off my bed so that the starving kids in other countries would have food to eat. I'm not sure where I came up with this idea, but when my mother found out, she sternly set me straight. *"God never wants you to suffer to feed another child,"* she said as she picked everything up off the floor. *"Let's make the bed. God loves you. He doesn't want you to suffer."*

I didn't say it at the time, but taking her words in, I wondered if she knew we were suffering because of Dad. His drinking binges and the family being terrorized in the wee hours of the morning definitely brought suffering to us. As a matter of fact, we all had circles under our eyes from crying and getting no sleep. I can still feel the defeat after those nights I thought would never end. My mother would drop me off at school on her way to work. My eyes were still wet with tears and the memories of him throwing things around and screaming all night.

My mother would look so sad, but all she'd say was, *"Have a good day and don't think about home at all. This is your time to forget all about it and have fun."* She'd wipe my tears and say, *"Smile."* It was almost a demand. She made sure I heard her too. *"I said forget all about Dad and last night. I want you to have a good day,"* she stated firmly.

Now, I wonder if she was saying that to make sure I wouldn't disclose our secret to others. She didn't need to worry about that. I didn't verbalize it to her, but I would never reveal our secret because it might mean being taken away from her. As I got out of the car, I would smile just so she would feel better about me and not worry. I wanted to make sure she was okay at her job.

When I was an adult and we could talk about these things, she confided that she had trained herself on how to forget home and do what she had to do to make a living for our family. She told me about her own exhaustion and how she snuck away on her morning breaks to take a nap in a secluded spot.

I did my best to follow my mother's instructions to *"forget home."* I disciplined myself to forget about those nights. I made every effort to enjoy those seven hours in an environment different than my home. It actually became a time of freedom. For a moment, I forgot our deep, dark secret. I forgot that I lived a life very different from the other children. I played the role of a normal kid quite well. I knew that I mustn't let on about my home life or we would all be in trouble.

I found great peace in the daily Catholic Mass at 8:00 a.m. Despite the ritual of kneeling, sitting, and standing, I fell asleep on many occasions. Of course the nuns were there to prod me awake and to remind me of my disrespect to God. I wonder why they never questioned why a little boy was so tired. As a student at St. David's Catholic School, we were obligated to show up at Sunday Mass. For my mother, Mass was a love she carried to her last days on this earth plane. Sunday Mass was boring for me, but it was a break from my father who never attended.

Even outside of Catholic school, the Church was a big part of my life. My mother was a devoted Catholic and I would attend Novenas with her on Wednesday nights. Novenas are prayers recited in Latin. It was boring to a little boy, but it was a safe place to sleep. I would curl up next to her and be lulled to sleep by the chanting. The words became a comforting and peaceful lullaby.

There were many different statues and pictures of Jesus in my home. My mother's favorite was the Infant Jesus of Prague. She bought it in 1954 in Germany and brought it with her back to the States. This statue represented Jesus as a child, elaborately dressed in a long flowing gown with a crown on his head. The nuns always told me Jesus was the Prince of Peace, and his Father, God, is the King. I loved that statue too. I felt a kinship to it. He was the Prince and I felt like a prince born of royalty. Even though it didn't out picture that way in the script of my life, still, it gave me hope that maybe someday I would realize this dream and find out that my father was really a king.

My mother had special prayers on the back of holy cards just for the Infant Jesus. Later, she would tell me it was her devotion and prayers to the Infant Jesus all those years that got her through her life with my father. Those statues remained with her until her death. After her death, I released most of her statues to different churches and people but I kept her favorite, the Infant Jesus. I can still see her kissing her finger and putting it to Jesus' lips as she walked by that statue.

My mother never discussed religion at home with my father. We did not pray at dinner because it would just have angered him. I believe his anger stemmed from his jealousy over my mother's relationship with Jesus and God. He didn't say he was jealous but he acted that way. Maybe it was because she was so obviously peaceful with God, and he was so tormented. I don't know the real answer but it gives me some kind of understanding of his deep, seething anger. He would make fun of her all the time, ridiculing her about her love for Jesus, while at the same time screaming that she was a whore.

I'm not sure how the Infant Jesus survived my father's jealousy when many of her other spiritual treasures did not. For example, my mother had one of those plastic statues of Jesus on the dashboard of our car. She said it was for protection while we were traveling. My father used it as an ashtray. My mother held in her rage, but she kept that statue of Jesus with the burnt face for years. In our dining room, we had another religious treasure from Germany. It was a big painting of Jesus at Gethsemane. Gethsemane was where Jesus spent his last night before his crucifixion. That painting was beautiful and gave me a lot of peace when I looked at it. However, peace was fleeting in our turbulent home and the peace of that painting would fade into chaos on one fateful night.

I am not sure what aggravated my father that particular night. His jealousy of my mother's relationship with Jesus was particularly acute. He was calling Jesus every filthy name he could come up with as my mother unsuccessfully tried to calm him down. "Jesus would never love a whore like you!" he screamed over and over.

I was crying for him to stop. My mother pleaded with her favorite phrase, "*I beg of you, Don, stop! I beg of you, don't!*"

I knew the night was about to get very dark. Yes, it would be one of our run-for-your-life nights. Why we didn't just leave right away, I don't know. I think we both felt that maybe we could turn him around. We stood frozen as he became more and more violent and out of control. Suddenly, he lunged toward the painting, putting his fist right through the glass as he punched Jesus over and over. "*Where is your Jesus now, Katie?*" he kept screaming over and over, as his voice mingled with the sound of broken glass hitting the floor. My father was now definitely gone and all that remained was a madman with a fist full of blood. Who was this man? Was he possessed like those stories I heard in religion class? He continued to taunt my mother as we stood in terror. "*There is no God to stop me now!*" he screamed.

You might wonder at times like these why we didn't call the police. Oh, we did, but all we would get were questions to my mother like, "*What did you do to aggravate your husband?*" I think we finally gave up on getting that kind of help. It was easier to just run, which we eventually always did.

As we stood frozen in disbelief, my father ran to the kitchen and came running out with a knife. The house was filled with a chorus of screams; his and ours. Was he coming for us? No, it was Jesus he was after. "*Here, Katie, watch this!*" he yelled out, as he stabbed the picture of Jesus repeatedly. "*Where is your Jesus now, Katie? How is all that praying working for you now?*" He continued to stab the painting.

The moment had come. It was time to get out! "*Danny, Frankie, grab your coats!*" my mother screamed. We were already running for the door.

"*Where do you think you're going?*" my father yelled with eyes wild and blood dripping from his hand. He waved the knife in rage. "*You aren't going anywhere you little bitch, get* back here."

Danny and I were already out the door. "*Get in the car now!*" Mom screamed to us, as she grabbed her coat and keys. Fleeing like refugees, off we went into the night, leaving that man I didn't recognize standing at the door screaming, "*Come back here now, whore! Where is your God now, Katie?*"

My mother drove off. The car was deafeningly still. There were no words. Even my brother Danny had nothing to say. I can't remember where we fled to that night. Did we just go for a drive? Did we get ice cream? Did we go to the movies? Did we spend the night at Nana's? I don't remember. However, I do recall returning with that dreadful fear in my stomach. What would we find? Would he still be awake? Would he still be mad? Would the father I knew be gone and this other person still here?

On this particular occasion we found him passed out on the floor surrounded by broken glass, furniture tipped over, and things tossed around. His hand was wrapped in a blood-soaked towel. The destroyed painting of Jesus was still hanging on the wall. All I could think was, "*My God, my father got away with stabbing Jesus! No lightning came to strike him. Where was God now? Did he even exist? Was Dad right, or had the King sacrificed his only son once again?*" These were the questions in a young boy's mind; questions that rang out with no answers.

We started picking things up and putting the crime scene back together again. My father finally woke up with the familiar look and response, "*What happened Katie?*" I ignored him once again, as my mother took him into the bathroom and bandaged his hand. I could hear him apologizing, "*What happened? I am sorry Katie,*" he kept repeating.

My father was back and the other person was tucked away for a moment, giving us just enough time to take a breath before he would return to torture us all over again. My mother put him to bed and then I watched her take that painting down. I assumed she got rid of it and the awful memory of that night. However, I wasn't aware at that time that her love for Jesus would never allow her to do that. I would find that out thirty years later.

The Resurrection

"You must let go of a thing for a new one to come to you."

- RALPH WALDO EMERSON

Years later when I was in my late twenties, I was on one of my frequent trips to visit my mother in the mobile home park where she still lived, and as I said, would continue to live in for over fifty years. I wondered why she'd never moved from that trailer where so much horror took place. She said she was happy and comfortable there. She often spoke of how safe she felt surrounded by the things that meant so much to her.

Familiarity, even in dysfunction, can sometimes bring a comfort that dominates the fear of change. That hard change would come later when my mother would eventually be forced to move from her beloved trailer. However, for now, maybe her comfort and feelings of safety came from knowing it was all hers without the drama of living with my father. (At this point, my father was institutionalized, which I will expand on later.)

My mother wasn't a hoarder, but she sure liked to keep things. Trying to get her to throw anything away was like ripping a toy from a child's hands. I had long given up on it even though her little mobile home was crowded to overflowing. Whenever I entered that home, I was like a little kid. My first stop was the refrigerator. Not that I wanted anything to eat, but I just liked to look and see what was there. What was her new food fad? I grabbed one of her twinkies and headed to the storage closet. I don't usually go through my mother's closets but I was looking for one of those old photo albums I wanted to take back to L.A. with me.

The closet was crowded with all kinds of memorabilia. Right next to my picture album there was something that looked like a rolled up poster. I unrolled it, expecting to find one of my teenage bubblegum idols. However, staring back at me was Jesus in Gethsemane, the painting that had been stabbed that horrible night so many years before. I stared at the knife slits and the dried-up drops of blood that had oozed out of my father's hand. A deep chill ran up my spine. The wounds in those knife marks were etched deeply in my own psyche. I couldn't fathom why my mother would have saved this. Did she even remember it was here? As I stared at it, my huge dark memory was suddenly taken over by something else. I could use this to do what I always loved to do – surprise my mother and bring her some joy. I would sneak it out of the house, take it back to Los Angeles and have it restored and give it to her for Christmas. I'm not sure how I knew it could be restored, but there was an urge within me to do so. In fact, it was already done in my mind. I thought that perhaps by even making the effort, I could restore a part of my mother's life that my father took away.

I had always taken on the vocation of restoring my mother's life. As I grew older, on Christmas I would do my best to fill the tree with presents to make up for the stories she told me of her Depression days and all the Christmases she experienced a giftless tree. One particular Christmas of her childhood was significant in the drama. It was the day her siblings and she learned that there was no Santa. Apparently, her brother, fourteen years her elder, was supposed to come

43

home with the Santa presents that Christmas. My mother and her siblings were told to stay up in their rooms until their mother called them down to open their presents. Well, you know how kids are on Christmas Day. The excitement pulls children out of bed well before dawn. My mother and her siblings were no different. They snuck downstairs to find no presents and empty stockings. Through no fault of his own, the brother had been delayed in his return with the presents. Although he finally did arrive later in the day, you can only imagine what a sad realization it was for those little children to discover there was no Santa.

That story stuck with me forever. It was no wonder in the moment of finding that demolished painting that the chief thought in the mind of the Little Man (who still existed in my psyche) was to restore the years my father had taken from her. It was a big responsibility but I was up for it. I snuck the painting out of the house and back to L.A. where I found someone to do the job. *"This painting isn't worth anything,"* the woman argued with me, *"And it's going to cost you at least $500 to have it repaired and reframed under glass."*

That was a steep price for a young, nonworking actor in L.A., but I would have to make it happen. Five-hundred dollars was a small amount in my mind to heal such a big wound for my mother. Can one restore the past as if nothing had ever happened? It was that challenge that moved me to reach into my wallet and take out the money I had saved for rent and place it on the counter. I convinced myself by thinking it was only the beginning of the month. I'd just work a little harder that month. The woman took the money, shaking her head, probably wondering what a handsome young man wanted with an old ripped painting of Jesus.

When I went back to get the painting, I was more than excited. It was restored perfectly. Finally, Christmas Eve arrived. I was packing for the trip up to my mother's. I took out the painting to wrap it. I smiled, thinking I had resurrected Jesus. He even looked better than he did before the crucifixion by my father. The frame was gold, ornate, and quite classy. It had a sense of richness that made it better than before. As Jesus's face began to be covered by my Christmas wrapping, I had an odd thought. It was something I hadn't thought about before. What if my mother had wanted to get rid of it? Maybe she forgot she'd left it in that closet? Would I hurt her by bringing up the past, and at Christmas of all times? In spite of those doubts, I kept wrapping it. As Jesus was finally tied in a Christmas bow, that money consciousness of my family rose to the top of my thoughts. For a moment, I felt like a fool. *"I spent $500 on something that cost my mother $20 in Germany,"* I chided myself. But the part of me that wanted to please my mother was stronger. *"No, I'm willing to take the chance."*

On Christmas morning as my mother ripped the paper back to expose the resurrected Jesus, I waited for her reaction. She was stunned, silent. As I watched her continue to let the painting sink in, I could feel a silent bond between the two of us, remembering that night so many years ago. When she finally spoke, her surprise was palpable. I believe she had forgotten that she had kept the painting. I explained how I had found it and why I had decided to restore it for her. She was so grateful, not so much for the return of the painting, but for my deep love for her. I don't remember everything we talked about but I was most definitely pleased with myself for having made the decision.

***

Many years later after my mother passed away and I was married to Rita and living on the island of Kaua`i, we returned to California to release some of my mother's belongings. There was nothing much left because she had downsized so many times. However, there it was— Jesus at Gethsemane. What were we going to do with it? It would just add to the already costly packing of things we needed to take with us over 2600 miles of ocean. Plus, we were now New Thought ministers. We certainly couldn't hang it in our Center on Kaua`i. We desperately tried to give it to several religious stores. No one wanted it. What happened to it? The picture that had become a fifty-year legend in my life's history, and now in a book, ended up in Burbank, California next to a dumpster. Rita and I justified what we did by convincing ourselves that someone would find it and enjoy it. We took one last picture of it as we ran into the night like two thieves. It didn't feel good to us but we did what we had to do. The question was, could I leave a history I wanted to forget by that dumpster too? I couldn't, nor did I want to. There is a difference between reliving and holding on to your history and just keeping the gems that made you the person you are. That painting was one of those gems and its memory would remain with me forever.

Leaving the House on Clinton Avenue

"Time to leave now, get out of this room, go somewhere, anywhere; sharpen this feeling of happiness and freedom, stretch your limbs, fill your eyes, be awake, wider awake, vividly awake in every sense and every pore. It is time to leave."

- PAULO COELHO

My father's paranoia came to a head one day at Clinton Avenue which led to the end of our life there. It happened just like this. As she always did after work, my mother picked me up from Nana's. This particular day as we made our way up the steep hill to our home, we noticed our street was blocked off by a police barricade. We were stopped by an officer. My mother rolled down her window. *"What's going on here, Sir?"*

I could tell my mother was nervous. The officer answered with a question, *"Where are you going, Ma'am?"*

"Home," she replied.

"What's your address?" the police officer asked with a serious look.

"It's right there! That is my house!" she replied frantically, as she pointed to our home.

As the officer peered closer into the car window, I started

47

to get those nervous jitters in my stomach. *"Do you know a man by the name of Donovan Engler?"* he asked.

"Yes, that's my husband. What's happened? Is he all right?" Her voice was desperate.

I could feel my stomach sink into the ground. *"Oh God,"* I thought, *"What now?"*

The officer didn't say anything. Instead, he ushered our car through the blockade. There, in front of our house was my handcuffed father. I saw our neighbors at their doors peeking out. They looked both afraid and curious. At this point, my fear was compounded by my embarrassment. Just like my mother, I cared deeply about what the neighbors thought. My mother got out of the car. The officer addressed her, *"We got an anonymous emergency call from a neighbor that a man was wandering around pointing a rifle at the houses, yelling and threatening them,"* explained the officer in a monotone voice.

All my mother could shout in response was, *"Where did he get the gun? My husband does not own a gun. I wouldn't allow a gun in my home."* At this point, she was hysterical.

"We traced it to Montgomery Wards. He bought it on credit," the officer stated flatly.

"Don't you have to have a license to own a gun?" my mother screamed. She was really upset but I could see she was trying to control herself. I was numb. I couldn't believe this was real. I felt like I was watching one of those cop shows you see on TV. The only difference was that those shows paled in comparison to this moment in my life. My only thought was how am I going to face the neighbors. I looked around wondering where Danny was. Where was he when we needed him? My fourteen-year-old brother must

have been out at one of his games. This was my burden and mine alone.

After some questioning and paperwork, they didn't arrest my father. The reason was because there were no bullets in the gun. "*He's all yours,*" the officer said, and then got into his car and drove away. The neighbors crowded in on us, and let my mother know how frightened they were by my father's behavior. "*We feared for our lives, for sure, Mrs. Engler!*"

My mother tried to placate them with some weak reason for my father's behavior. She said something like, "*Sorry, he hasn't been himself lately.*" Then she made some kind of false promise, letting them know he had a doctor appointment soon. Of course, none of it was true. Doctor appointments wouldn't come till much later. The neighbors slowly broke up their gaping party and went back into their homes. My father had already gone into the house. My mother rushed into the house with me in tow. Boy, did she give my father a piece of her mind. He made some lame excuse and opened a beer. My mother ignored him, snatched the empty gun and dragged me out to the car. She drove as fast as she could to Montgomery Wards. She made her way to the weapons department. Slamming the gun down on the counter, she chewed out the store manager. "*How could you just give a gun to someone without checking them?*" she screamed. "*Here's my credit card and I want a refund!*" The clerk credited her card but said nothing to answer her question. There weren't any laws in those days. To date, nothing much has changed. At the writing of this book, gun violence and mass shootings are very common. Being able to easily acquire a gun without an adequate background check is one of the causes.

I shiver at the different ending my story could have had, and how my life and my family's life might have been so different had there been bullets in that gun. How grateful I am as I tour through these memories that no one got killed. How grateful I am to be here to write about it. I marvel at this young boy who maneuvered himself through the minefield of mental illness, and not only survived, but eventually, emotionally thrived.

I didn't know it at the time, but I know now. There is something called Grace that protects us in instances like this one. It's the deepest and truest part of ourselves that comes to our aid. The purpose of Grace is to protect us when we can't consciously do it for ourselves. It's the bottom to our grief. The more we become attuned and surrender to it, the more it uses us. I believe I was very attuned to Grace on a deep level in those days. It was that little boy's belief in the saints and prayer. It was his faith in a Higher Power.

My father, on the other hand, didn't know anything about Grace. He was merely deeply disturbed and suffered from an undiagnosed disease without the help he needed. However, I firmly believe Grace did work through him. That better part of himself came through to protect him and us. As my story unfolds you will see, it happened in other instances too.

That very night, our exit from Clinton Avenue began. With no thought about what had really happened, my father merely whined at my mother, "*Katie, we need to move. I tell you it's because the neighbors don't like me. I promise I'll be better if we move. I won't drink as much. Please let's move!*"

And again, eventually, my mother gave in. We were like fugitives constantly running, making one bad decision after another, while living in the fog of an undiagnosed mental illness. I might not have liked my father and his craziness, as we called it in those days, but I loved those three years in the East Richmond Heights on Clinton Avenue. I was deeply sad that we had to leave. I also had another reason to be sad.

I didn't mention it before, but in addition to our little dog, Mitty, we had an outdoor dog, Coleen, a beautiful German Shepherd. I loved Coleen but we had to give her up because she was way too big for our next life in a mobile home park. Luckily, Nana had a big backyard and agreed to take Coleen, and thankfully, we could keep Mitty.

Thinking of my old house, I wonder if that is why I love living in big homes. Even now, with just my wife and myself, we live in a four-bedroom house. Perhaps it is my way of making it up to my inner child who went through so much back then. I do believe it's never too late to have another childhood.

I recently returned to Clinton Avenue for my fiftieth grade school reunion. The house that seemed so large at the time appeared dwarfed compared to my memory of the huge horrific experiences that turned my life upside down at that address. As I looked back at the move away from Clinton, I do remember feeling a sense of relief about the possibility that my father would not humiliate us anymore. Could I finally release the embarrassment I felt on that day he held the neighborhood hostage? Maybe we could start over and be a normal family. I knew the chances were slim and I'd more than likely be disappointed by my father's empty promises, but I tried my best to keep optimistic about the future.

***

I'm sure the choice to move to a mobile home park instead of another house was my mother's idea. As I've stated before, a mobile home was her preferred abode. I do remember the day we went shopping. She was super excited. After purchasing a new mobile home, we needed to choose a park. In those days, they were very particular about who they let in. Both my mother and father happened to know the manager of the Circle S Coral Mobile Home Park. He knew about my father's ups and downs, but he pulled some strings to get us in. The manager of the Circle S Coral was a brother Moose too. My parents belonged to the Order of the Moose and the Moose took care of their own. We were definitely in.

I didn't know that mobile home parks had a stigma about them. Deep down inside, I still felt like a prince. However, I would soon come to realize I was the kid who went from the big house in Richmond Heights to a trailer park on San Pablo Avenue. I would also come to terms with the truth that my father would never get better and we would never be a normal family. I tried to rethink it all and make some sense of why this was happening to me. I had read the stories of Siddhartha. Maybe I was leaving my kingdom on the hill to discover why there was suffering in the world. This is how I chose to think about my life even at a young age. I knew that life could be better because it must be better than it was showing itself to be. My ability to cling to optimism became my inner savior.

The Great Protector

"Being brave doesn't mean you are not scared; it just means you do the scary thing anyway."

- Rose McGowan

It was like a siren in the night, a voice screaming my mother's name, *"Katie, Katie, Katie! Where the hell are you? Get your ass in here!"*

That was my cue. I was on call any time I heard my father's voice screaming like that. It was part of those violent rages that came when he was drunk. He was six foot four and I was no match for him physically, but there were other ways to fight the giant. Intuitively, I found those ways through trial and error. I was seven years old when I took on the role of the great appeaser, or as I liked to think of myself, *"The Great Protector."*

I had a calming effect on my father and I used this power. As the years went on, I perfected this superpower of actually stopping him from raging. As I look back on it, it was a form of manipulation, but it assisted me in protecting my mother. My one goal in life was to stop my father from hurting my mother. What if something happened to her? If he killed her, and sometimes it looked like he certainly wanted to, what would happen to me and my brother? No matter what I had to do, I could never let that happen. So, on many occasions, when my mother was watching one of her sports games on TV and that desperate cry came from my father, she'd call to me, "*Can you appease your father?*" I always obliged.

The room was always dark, and that familiar stale smell of alcohol always permeated the air. There he would be, sprawled out on the bed in his undershorts and tee shirt. "*Dad, Dad?*" I spoke in a calm, quiet voice. As I moved closer to the bed, I took a reading of his state of mind. My intuitive powers were strong. Had he passed out? I wasn't sure, but I'd continue to creep toward that huge figure in the dark. I did not turn on the lights because I couldn't take the chance of waking him up fully. My mission was to get him to fall asleep. As you've read so far, my father had a habit of passing out after the alcohol and rage wore him down a bit. We all looked forward to these golden moments. The family could breathe and even relax, if relaxing were ever possible in our household.

As I stood there in the dark by the bed, I could tell he was definitely in that state where I knew he couldn't get up or hurt me. I crawled into the bed and began my way of soothing him to sleep. The smell of liquor was hot on my face. He knew it was me and he'd begin the monologue I knew well. "*Your mom doesn't understand me like you do. That bitch, she's no good,*" he'd ramble on, calling her awful names. I'd just listen. I was a good listener for a little boy. I would carry this skill into adulthood. He kept calling my mother names but I wasn't going to argue with him. That would be too dangerous. My only purpose was to calm him down so he would go back to sleep. I put my hand to his forehead and began stroking it and calling him by the name I reserved for these occasions. "*Pappo,*" I whispered, "*Mom isn't trying to be mean and you are not bad. You just get a little scary when you get mad. No one is against you, especially Mom. We just get scared, that's all.*"

I continued to stroke his hair and face. He was definitely

calming down. He began rubbing his rough beard on the side of my face. *"You're the only one who understands me, loves me. Not even Danny understands me like you do."*

"Danny loves you, Pappo. Mom doesn't hate you." I kept my voice really quiet.

He was becoming more and more relaxed. My apprehension began to fade away. He'd be asleep soon. I knew it. It always worked. I waited for my moment to escape but he held my face against his. *"You're a real good boy. You understand me. You're a real good boy. You're the only one I really love."* He was holding me like a teddy bear and I was really uncomfortable. He began to move his lips around my face. The smell of alcohol was almost suffocating. He continued to rub his beard against my face. Those stubbles were so rough, I got many beard rashes on my face on those occasions.

I was confused by my feelings. I was curious why my body felt strange, like I was dropping down an elevator shaft. Why did it feel good and scary at the same time? I wanted to pull away but my body was like rubber. It felt good to have this strange control over my father. I was weakened and powerful at the same time. Finally, he fell asleep. That was my moment to escape. Quietly as I could, I crawled out of the bed and tiptoed out of the room. At least for now, I'd done my job.

This was a ritual I got used to between the ages of seven and twelve. I was not always successful getting him to stay in that bedroom, but as the years went on, my track record as the Great Protector became quite good. However, I always left feeling confused by the odd feelings my body had when I would lie in that bed with him. These feelings weighed heavily on a young boy's mind, but were outweighed by my resolve to protect my family from this dangerous wild man.

Contemplating it as an older adult, I came to the conclusion that on those occasions, in some way, I took on my mother's role in their bed. As I grew into adulthood, I had much confusion to unravel. I would someday have to face the sexual overtone of these experiences with my father. Although he never penetrated me, it was clear that something sexual was happening. As an adult, my mother shared with me that my father had been impotent for many years of their marriage. I understood that these bedroom encounters could have been totally different if that weren't so. I choose to think of it as Divine Intervention or that gift of Grace I spoke of earlier.

As I look back at myself as a little boy, I feel I was quite special. How did I manage to turn out somewhat normal? Did I come here with these gifts of resilience or did I acquire them by mere survival? In therapy, I realized these experiences with my father were why I had such a hard time with puberty. I never felt like the other men I saw. Puberty is difficult as it is, and mine was compounded by my emotionally playing the role of a wife. I surmise I also took on my father's insecurity about his manhood. As a prepubescent boy who had not fully come to understand the male and female identities, I was operating energetically in both. Although I knew I had to do it to survive, I was left in a state of both confusion and curiosity.

As I have reparented myself for many years, I have thought, "*What an incredible little boy I was to create the way to enter into the psyche of a mad man. What a genius this little boy was!*"

Behind closed doors, our family was living in a self-made sanitorium. I have to say, I was angry and tired. It was like working several full-time jobs. Fortunately, I would finally have occasional breaks when my father was medicated or have a stint in a mental hospital. My necessity to keep my father calm and all of us safe birthed the Patrick that would eventually choose to experience rebirthing therapy. What is rebirthing therapy? Let me take you back to my thirties.

I was living in New York City in the late eighties and going through what I lovingly call the "Shirley MacLaine and *Out on a Limb*" period of my life. Since not all of my readers will get this reference, let me call it my *"New Age"* time of life. Many of us were experimenting with all the new ways of becoming enlightened: crystals, channeling, psychics, palm readings, astrological charts, and chakra cleansing were just a few. I was quite interested in the modality of rebirthing.

> *"Rebirthing (RT) is an unconventional form of bodywork and mind/body psychotherapy, developed in the 1970s by Leonard Orr, based on the belief that the trauma of birth has lifelong consequences on a person's psyche, as the infant passes from the warm safety of the womb to the cold vast world. In RT, the client is guided through a reenactment of birth with hyperventilation (termed conscious connected breathing), which releases tension said to have begun at birth; an individual's expression of this repressed trauma is said to facilitate healing of physical mental and emotional disorders."*
>
> - SEGEN'S MEDICAL DICTIONARY.
> © 2012 FARLEX, INC. ALL RIGHTS RESERVED.

> *"Rebirthing is a very therapeutic technique used in various types of alternative medicine and psychotherapy. Rebirthing generally refers to a technique used to treat a patient who has suffered some traumatic event. The idea*

is to simulate a second birth, thus creating a fresh start, a fresh consciousness in the life and mind of the patient. Although this second birth may be achieved in a number of ways, the basis of the therapy holds that revisiting the trauma experienced during birth can have a therapeutic effect." (wisegeek.com)

Several people I knew had tried rebirthing and they said good things about it, or at least said it was worth a try. When one of my friends explained it to me, he told me he drooled a little bit out of the corner of his mouth and his hands curled like an infant. He assured me the first couple of times were pretty mild. It was all about releasing any memories of trauma or anything that would be stuck in my cellular system. He recommended a person he'd gone to that I had seen on late night local TV. I was definitely still a seeker and I thought, *"Why not?"* I made an appointment for a rebirthing session.

The man worked out of his apartment. I was a little apprehensive about this, but since I'd seen him on TV talking about New Age and other metaphysical topics, I convinced myself it was safe to go. The day arrived. When I met him in person, he seemed much younger than his television persona, but then, I was young too. We sat and talked a bit and he outlined what we would be doing. *"I will guide you all the way through. No worries. You are safe in my hands."* He reiterated that the rebirthing technique was created by Leonard Orr. *"It is quite simple, he said. You'll lie down on the floor and follow my breathing directions."*

He explained that it was all about releasing trauma slowly and it would probably take more than one session. However, he didn't know me. I could never do anything halfway. We began the process. I started to breathe. It went on a while and I began to feel like I was hyperventilating. "*Just breathe deeper and let it go,*" he instructed.

I continued to feel light headed. The next thing I knew, my back arched uncontrollably and I felt as though my stomach was huge and sticking out.

"*Oh my God! What is happening?*" I screamed out. Suddenly, I felt like my penis disappeared and I felt an opening in its place, like a vagina.

"*Keep breathing,*" he insisted.

Oh my God! I felt like I was giving birth. I could feel me opening wider and wider. I kept crying out, "*What's happening?*" as I continued to arch my back uncontrollably. My back was really hurting.

"*Get it out of me! Get it out of me!*" I screamed, as I grabbed at my facilitator's hand and squeezed.

I felt delirious, scared, and confused. "*What is going on? Oh My God!*"

"*Push!*" he repeated over and over.

I felt like this would never end. I was crying, screaming, cussing, sweating, and I almost felt like I was going to die. It felt like whatever was inside me wasn't going to come out.

"*Get it out of me! Please!*" I screamed.

It felt like a final push was taking place. Whatever was inside of me was most definitely coming out. I even felt what they call the afterbirth expelled from my body. Something moved out from inside of me. It was a baby. This was a physical sensation — not a vision. I was totally awake and present. I was finally relieved, but my legs were still spread so wide. I began to laugh hysterically from the release of such pressure and pain. I looked between my legs. I could see a baby boy. I knew it was me. His hair shimmered like diamonds on a lake. I spoke out, "*The Prince is born, the Prince is born! I am so glad you are here!*"

As I started to reach for the baby, I went into the fetal position and became the baby. When I started to become more present and in my body, I reached down to make sure I still had a penis. It was there. I felt naked, yet I was fully-clothed. As I came back from the experience, I looked up and saw my facilitator.

"*What the hell just happened?*" I asked.

He didn't answer. I don't think he heard me. He looked like he had seen a ghost. He asked, "*What happened just now, and what did you mean the Prince is born?*"

I was shocked by his question. "*I was hoping you could tell me,*" I responded. "*Aren't you in charge?*"

He informed me that something like this had never happened with a client before. He had never heard of anyone, especially a man, experiencing what I experienced. I asked him what he saw.

"*I witnessed you having a baby,*" he said with a shaking voice.

I wondered if he thought the Prince was a dark thing like the devil or something. We talked a bit and I told him about how I had always felt I had a hard time getting here to earth. I felt I had been aborted many times. After our debriefing, I left his apartment. It was an odd feeling leaving him after we had gone through such an experience together. I felt a strange intimacy with him.

I don't think he ever checked on me and I never went back. I never did another rebirthing either. I had no Google Search in those days, and I could not find others who had had the same experience. I felt alone and different, and yet I felt I was very special to go to such extremes to legitimize my birth and the validity for my existence. I later contacted a reputable institute in California that studied and documented rebirthing. The simplest explanation I received was that I had reached both polarities of male and female and had birthed myself.

As I contemplate my childhood and how I took on the role of both husband and wife to my parents, it does not surprise me that I was able to create such an event for myself. The remembrance I have of being inside my mother's womb and wanting to prove I was worthy of being born, even though it would cause her such fear, pain, and shame, makes my rebirthing experience make even more sense. I am still not sure I've fully processed that experience with the true integrity that it required. I've told few people about it, and I'm not sure those I have told truly believed me. It doesn't matter. I know what happened. It's been thirty years since that experience and I am no longer in my "New Age/Shirley MacLaine" state of mind, but I do believe that by rebirthing myself that day, I gave myself permission to be here. I have always felt like a prince that lost his way and that day was my homecoming.

Just Another
Christmas

"He was still too young to know that the heart's memory eliminates the bad and magnifies the good, and that thanks to this artifice we manage to endure the burden of the past."

- GABRIEL GARCÍA MÁRQUEZ

My father didn't get better after moving from Clinton Avenue; in fact, he got worse. The worse he got, the more I became the Little Man until the day when I decided that taking care of myself was more important. However, that day would come much later, and after many more turbulent times like that Christmas of my tenth year.

It was my self-assigned responsibility to lead the way in creating the best holidays possible, especially Christmas. I worked overtime to make sure our family experienced what I thought of as Christmas joy. I had my own small savings account just for gifts. I put myself in charge of decorating the tree, wrapping presents, sending Christmas cards, shopping, and playing music. I loved Christmas! No matter what drama might have been occurring in our home, I would make sure Christmas survived. However, it was an almost impossible task because the holidays brought about more drinking than any time of year. There were parties overflowing with eggnog and brandy and other traditional drinks. I wondered if other families experienced anything like we did when my father's other personality came out to visit. I didn't know, nor did I care, when it came to Christmas. In our home behind the family drama, the Christmas spirit remained alive and well with me. Looking back, I can see I was almost desperate to make sure Christmas happened.

One of my favorite responsibilities was trimming the tree. If it had been up to me, I would have had that Christmas tree up by Thanksgiving but my mother insisted waiting until December 15th to buy our tree. She said she wanted to make sure it would last until January 6th which was the Catholic holiday, the Epiphany. The Epiphany represented the day the Three Wise Men visited the Baby Jesus. That's what the story said anyway. Most Catholics kept their Christmas decorations up until then and we weren't any different.

We had one of those cardboard fireplaces that were very popular during those years. We didn't have a lot of money but those fireplaces made me feel rich. As tacky as it seems to me now, at the time, I thought that cardboard fireplace was the coolest thing in our mobile home. You see, I didn't think of myself as upper or lower class. I knew we struggled financially, but I didn't feel poor. I felt rich in so many ways, unlike my brother, Danny, who was always ashamed of his family's status. I think it was because he went to an all-boys private high school where the majority of kids were wealthy. Danny was so embarrassed by our family that before he was old enough to drive, he would have his friends pick him up away from the mobile home park so they wouldn't know where we lived. On the other hand, I would bring kids over to the house even when my father was drunk or having one of his crazy moments.

My mother would ask me, *"Why in God's name do you let your friends see your dad like that?"*

"I'm not going to ruin my childhood, Mom. I want friends," I insisted. As I got older, I let her know that I hungered for a normal life and I was going to at least attempt to have one.

The Christmas tree trimming of my tenth year will be etched in my memory forever. It was the night my faith that my father would ever get better was replaced with hopelessness. As you will see by this story, that despair made me even more determined than ever to win this war against our family. I was extra excited that particular Christmas because my older friend, Jackie, was coming to dinner to be part of the festivities. Jackie knew about my father's drinking but she didn't care. She was going through a lot of her own pain. Her real mother deserted her because she had too many kids to care for. Her grandma and grandpa took Jackie in, but when her grandma died, her grandpa went on a drinking binge. Jackie was finally put in a foster home. Ironically, we were like a real family to her. My mother nurtured Jackie. In fact, she nurtured many of my friends. The details are hazy but my friends always said they could talk honestly to my mother because she didn't judge them.

Before Jackie's arrival at our house that night, I made sure everything was ready. Frank Sinatra was crooning traditional carols from the record player while I created the appetizers. I can still taste that squeezed cheddar cheese on Ritz crackers and the sliced real salami. We knew it was real salami because it was wrapped in white skin. It was a gift from my mother's work every Christmas along with a box of See's Candy. Both treats were saved especially for the Christmas tree trimming night. By the time Jackie arrived, the scene was set. It would be nothing less than a Hallmark Christmas, topped with a beautiful angel for the crowning of the tree. My father seemed to be on his best behavior but I was apprehensive. That lingering fear of his dangerous personality taking over was always present right in the pit of my stomach. Still, I opted for a whole night of joy. "*Please God!*" I thought.

We were laughing and having a good time, when the Seagram 7 and Seven-Up came out. I remember thinking, "*Why don't they just stick to beer?*" Why did special occasions in our family have to include "the hard stuff" and why was it called hard stuff anyway— or spirits? It wasn't very spiritual. Still, that night, even with the presence of alcohol, my determination for the best Christmas ever persevered.

Immediately after our dinner, Jackie and I could hardly wait to decorate the tree. I had already pulled out the bulbs, strings of light, candy canes, tinsel, and stockings with our names on them. Everything was laid out perfectly. Even our dog, Mitty, had her own stocking. Mitty stayed close by, watching the activities. As my father started to get more inebriated, like always, my hypervigilance kicked into gear. I knew my worst fears were soon to be realized. Even though he wasn't loud or disruptive, I knew it was coming. He began licking his lips and his face took on that familiar expression of meanness that accompanied those times. The evening would soon take a turn for the worst. There was nothing I could do but do my best to keep the cheer going. We continued to decorate the tree through the looming tension. Of course my mother knew trouble was brewing too. She began cleaning up, trying to keep the mood light, while at the same time attempting to give Dad attention. She wasn't as good as I was at keeping him calm, but that night, I was determined not to step in and take that role. As I was getting older, my patience for appeasing him was fading.

We were done decorating. The tree was beautiful. My mother praised our job and let Jackie know how happy she was to have her with us. We turned off the lights and stood back to get the full effect of the tree's beauty. The moment was silent and peaceful. Then suddenly, my father roared with the ferocity of a lion, "*Turn on the Goddamn lights!*"

I spoke softly. "*Dad, we're just enjoying the tree.*"

My mother jumped in, "*Don, please... I beg of you. We have company. Jackie's here.*"

"*I don't give a fuck and she can get the hell out of my house if she doesn't like it,*" he slurred.

"*I'm so sorry, Jackie,*" I whispered.

His voice boomed through the room at me. "*What are you whispering about, you little cocksucker?*"

I was yelling at him now. "*You ruin everything. You always ruin everything!*"

I could tell Mitty was getting scared. She began to whimper and whine. I stood in front of her because I was afraid my father would hurt her. However, he didn't care about the dog. He was focused on my mother. My father was the king of insults and they were always aimed at my mother. Tree trimming night was no different.

"*You're ugly,*" he taunted her. "*How could I have married someone as ugly as you and with a hooked nose? You look old enough to be my mother, old woman!*" He always called her old woman when his insults started. Then he started insulting Jackie, saying awful things about her family and calling her ugly and homely. We'd experienced this scene many times and we always knew the moment when it was time to get out of the house. That time had most definitely come. We knew it because he began to sing the old army song.

My mother grabbed the keys, "*Get in the car,*" she

commanded under her breath as she motioned us toward the door.

I grabbed Mitty's chain. I certainly wasn't going to leave her with him. Jackie started crying. I was crying. I was angry. I yelled at him, "*You ruined another Christmas. You always ruin everything, I hate you, I hate you!*"

My mother pushed us toward the door while I kept screaming at him. My father started lunging after me, "*You little bastard, don't you talk to me that way!*"

My mother turned back toward him and jumped between us. "*Don, stop it! We are taking Jackie home.*"

He was oblivious to us now, just stumbling around the room. "*All of you, get out! Fuck all of you,*" he yelled.

We moved out the door and toward the car. My mother turned back toward him, whispering loudly, "*Please, Don, you are disturbing the neighbors!*"

Disturbing the neighbors was a given in a mobile home park. There is four feet or less between trailers. You are so close, people can hear you sneeze.

"*Fuck these neighbors! They are all cocksuckers, and they're out after me, all those dirty sons-of-bitches,*" he screamed out the door, defiantly.

We were getting into the car while he continued to ramble, "*Shut this goddamn music off!*" We heard his voice melding with Frank Sinatra's in an eerie harmony until the sound of the needle scratching across the record ended that song in a deathly silence. All the car doors were locked and the windows were rolled up but we couldn't block out the song we hated the most. It was the old army song he always sang at times like these. He knew we hated it. Was it part of his inner rage pointed at us?

"Fuck 'em all, Fuck 'em all, the rich and the poor, I like to go swimming with fucked up old women. Fuck 'em all, fuck 'em all."

Over and over again, all through my childhood, he would sing that song until he passed out. We drove away, knowing this time would be no different. Eventually, he would lose consciousness.

As my mother drove, she remained amazingly calm on the exterior. I think it was because Jackie was there. She apologized to me and to Jackie, who was sobbing. Like I said before, Jackie had experienced her own family drama. We drove around for a while until we were able to calm Jackie down. Then, we dropped her off at the foster home. I'm not sure how long my mother and I drove but eventually we turned around and headed back home. If there was one thing worse than being kicked out of the house or fleeing from my father's rage, it was returning home. We never knew what we would find. My stomach would go into knots as we turned down our street and got closer to the trailer. That night, the trailer was dark and the lights outside were off. We could hardly make it out but there was something in front of our house in the middle of the street. Was it Dad? No. It was our Christmas tree! I swallowed my tears back hard. My father had thrown my beautiful Christmas tree out in the street!

"Mom, Mom, he threw our beautiful tree in the street. I hate him, I hate him!" I kept screaming. I began to sob, *"Mom, our tree is ruined. He ruined our tree!"*

My mother parked the car. She was silent, broken, tired. She looked at the tree but didn't say a thing. I think she was more interested in what was going on inside the house. We slowly moved toward the door and peered into the dark house. We heard that sweet sound of peace – my father snoring. Our experiences of the past let us know he would be out cold in the bedroom. Usually, this sound relieved me but tonight I felt something unfamiliar. It was a deep, seething anger. I had never felt this kind of anger towards him before. It scared me because I felt out of control.

As we entered the house, we scanned the room for damage. There was the usual mess of furniture turned over and scattered household items on the floor but nothing else was destroyed.

It appeared my father's only vengeance was on that tree out in the street. My mother looked at me with that lost look. *"Frankie, throw the tree out and please sweep up those bulbs and lights before the neighbors drive over them."*

"I have it handled, Mom. Just go to bed."

I took my place of authority as the Little Man and protector. My mother hesitated for just a moment, then relented and disappeared into the bedroom. As soon as she left, I ran back out into the street with a broom. I stood and stared at that twisted tree with broken bulbs and candy canes all over the ground. I began to sweep. My anger turned into the motion of the broom. It was as if I was sweeping up all the joy I had felt designing my perfect Christmas tree and then dumping it into the garbage. Right then, something changed in me. With every clank of broken bulbs and glass that hit the garbage can, my tears of anger turned into determination. I made a decision. I knew what I had to do. I would put that tree back together. *"You cannot destroy Christmas,"* I sobbed out loud.

In my desperation to save Christmas, I pulled the tree out from the street and dragged it into the house. Still seething with anger and determination, I wasn't hoping I could restore Christmas; I knew I would. I took my place once again as the protector of good. Little did I know, this role would be deeply embedded in my psyche until finally I would reveal it as cause for later dysfunction in my relationships. But that would be much later when I was an adult. For now, my task was to restore the damage my father had done.

Yes, the vision in my head of my father waking up in the morning to see that no one can destroy Christmas made the straightening of every branch and untwisting and re-tying of every piece of tinsel a work of deep satisfaction. The background sound of my father's snoring gave me a sense of relief and disgust at the same time. *"How could he get away with this?"* was my only thought. *"Why can't this just stop?"*

In that moment, the sound of his snoring blew a coldness around my heart. I found myself for the first time wishing he were dead, gone. How much better life would be without him torturing my mother, brother, and me. Was this the feeling that leads one to desperate measures? I was too young to know, but as the snoring got louder, I thought the most desperate thought I'd ever had. I could end this torture. All it would take was one knife and a stab to his heart. I could do it while he was sleeping and this nightmare could be over. I could end this bad dream once and for all.

My ten-year old mind was trembling with confusion. I went into the kitchen and got a knife. Shaking, I crept slowly toward the bedroom and stood at the closed door, grasping that knife for an endless moment. Tears streamed down my face. I slowly turned the knob, opened the door, and peered into the darkness. My mother and father were both asleep. I wondered how my mother could be asleep next to that man after all he'd done to us. It didn't matter. I would save her and myself. Suddenly, I stopped. I stood there at the door, frozen in my defeat. I couldn't do it. I was not a murderer, and yet the idea that I could have killed him gave me a sense of power. All at once, I somehow deeply understood that there were always options, no matter how bad it got. I was at choice, and killing him wasn't one of those. I wasn't trapped. I would someday be free from him. I don't know how I knew all of this. Maybe my belief in all those saints and apostles whispered the higher road in my ear. Maybe it was Grace that had saved me then, as it had so many times. Maybe I knew that act would make it even worse for my mother. My strong belief and faith in an invisible power I called God gave me that pinhole of light I needed to go on. I knew that eventually the nightmare would end. Holding my breath in fear that I would wake them, I slowly backed away from the door and returned the knife to the kitchen. I knew there was nothing I could do now except put the tree back together and move on.

Later in life when I would hear of someone accused of murder claiming self-defense, I would recall that moment standing outside my parents' door. I understood how one could be driven to such madness. I also felt so blessed that it was not in my makeup to kill. How different my life would be today!

I began to put the tree back together with a sense of peace. I restored what my father had destroyed. This was a resurrection, my resurrection of Christmas. Crucifixion and resurrection seemed to always play out in the events of my childhood with my father. When I was finished I turned out all the lights. I just sat there on the couch with my dog, Mitty, staring at that tree I'd brought back to life. My tears and anger had subsided. As the lights twinkled and the angel at the top seemed to smile at me, I felt a deep sense of satisfaction knowing the Christmas spirit had not died; it could never die. We all hold that spirit in our own hearts. That night, I was a part of bringing the joy of Christmas back and it would never leave me again.

The next morning my mother was so impressed and thankful for what I had done. I, in turn, could barely look at my father. He asked those questions he so often asked after nights like that when he couldn't understand why I was going out of my way to ignore him. *"What're you mad about? What happened?"* he asked.

There was an innocence in his voice that was almost pitiful. He did not remember a thing, while I was left with that memory for a lifetime. Much later, as an adult, I would have to look at it again and decide whether I could find the gift in it or just remain angry forever. It might have been just another Christmas but it would change my feelings for my father forever.

You might be wondering why my brother does not have a role in this Christmas memory. By that time, Danny was in the United States Marine Corp. He enlisted right after high school at age seventeen. My mother did not want him to go into the service, especially with the Vietnam War going on, but Danny convinced Dad to sign for him. He left for Vietnam right after he threw his high school cap in the air on graduation day. My brother and I shared many Christmas memories, but this one was mine and mine alone to experience.

Love Does Win!

"Love is a Cosmic force whose sweep is irresistible."
- ERNEST HOLMES

When my father was out of work, which was a lot of the time, he would be at home when I got out of school. My mother, of course, was at her full-time job. I never knew what to expect when I arrived home, as I never knew what state of mind he would be in — or out of.

I remember a particular day at age seven that would stand out in my mind for the rest of my life. As I walked around the corner, turning onto the street that led to our mobile home, a familiar rush of uncertainty filled my body. My stomach tightened and my palms began to sweat, the hair stood up on the back of my neck. It was not the first time I felt this kind of fear, but this day seemed different somehow. My imagination ran wild with the dreadful anticipation of what might lie ahead. Everything within me screamed *"Danger!"*

However, in spite of everything within me screaming for me to go the other direction, I kept walking toward home. My hypervigilance, better known as my Spidey senses, went into full gear and my protective shield went up. As I climbed the small set of stairs leading to the front door, my heart was beating out of my chest. With shaking hands, I put my key into the lock. Opening the door slowly, I called out into the darkened house, *"Dad, are you home?"*

The silence echoed off the dark walls. My voice quivered

as I called out again, "*Dad, are you here?*"

Slowly and cautiously, I walked through the door into the blackened room. The curtains were all pulled shut. There was a thin crack of afternoon light peeking through the drapes, revealing my father sitting in a chair, his back to me. He was so still and silent, for a moment I wondered if he was passed out or if he was dead. Either would have been a relief right now. With my eyes on both him and the door behind me, I walked toward the chair as quietly as I could. I accidently bumped into the table, alerting him of my presence. He slowly turned toward me. I was terrified. I felt like one big goosebump but I stood frozen. He looked straight at me and through me. Yes, it was my father in looks alone. His essence was something else. With tears of fear in my eyes I mumbled, "*Dad, are you OK? What's wrong, Dad?*"

He just kept staring at me. "*You're scaring me, Dad.*" I began to cry. "*You're scaring me. Please, say something!*" I was begging him by now.

He continued to stare right through me, looking almost hypnotized. I was paralyzed now, staring back at a man who was definitely not my father. The door wasn't that far. I mentally planned my escape. I could surely beat him to the door. I began to slowly back away. I could tell he was struggling to speak to me. In a slow slurred speech, he screamed, "*Get out, please get out, run, Frankie, run! They want me to hurt you. They want me to do bad things to you.*"

His voice got louder, urgent, and somewhat desperate. "*Get out now! They want me to hurt you!*"

As I backed away, I screamed out, "*OK Dad, OK! I am going.*"

As if a saber tooth tiger was chasing me, with tears in

my eyes and never looking back, I ran for my life into the afternoon light. Breathing, sweating, crying, I reached the familiar telephone booth at Rose and Mike's Liquor store on San Pablo Avenue. I had a pocket full of dimes for times like these. With shaking hands, I put the dime into the phone, and I called my mother at work. I remember the number to this day: 653-2933. If she couldn't pick me up, I'd go to my Nana's who lived quite a bit farther away. Either way, I was safe for now.

Years later, I have come to understand all the terror I felt on that afternoon had a different meaning and message. I realize unconditional love broke through the demons of my father's tormented mind and rescued a seven-year-old boy. I choose to believe my real father, Donovan Engler, came out long enough to save me from the many voices and personalities that tortured him. I do believe that love is more powerful than the darkness of mental illness. The philosopher and mystic, Ernest Holmes, wrote, "*Love is a Cosmic Force whose sweep is irresistible.*" I felt that Force that afternoon.

Freeing Moses

"I take my hand back, like a leaf letting go. It hurts too much to hang on. So why does it hurt so much to let go?"

- EMILY MURDOCH

"Please know I love you, my dumpster baby. I found you and cleaned you from the dirty dumpster of life. It is no longer safe for you to be with me so I must set you free. You are like Moses that was freed in the river and was taken downstream to safety. I cannot go with you because I must stay here and protect my mom. I love you so much and your safety is the most important thing to me. I pray for your safety and know that God will guide your little boat. I miss you already."

- THE LITTLE MAN

The coping skills I discovered and applied to survive my more than confusing childhood are ones for the mental health record books. Did I come here with these skills, or did they evolve moment-to-moment in the chaos? As I have already written, this is a question I still ponder. Although I wouldn't admit it at the time, there was the hidden me that wanted to be free from my father and my crazy family. In fact, at times I felt I must have been born into the wrong family.

But as frightening as my father could be, I knew I had to

stay. I had to protect my mother and my brother at any cost. Could that be the reason I was sent here and the reason I didn't try to escape?

When you don't have control, and I had none in my world, I believe you create it somehow, even if it is a false illusion of safety and security. It is the only way I can explain the following story.

***

On hot summer days, I would often spend time at this creek near our trailer park. (Excuse me. My mother would correct me here. "*It was a mobile home park, Patrick!*") I loved the creek near our "mobile home park" and spent a lot of time there. That creek felt like a whole secret world without having to stray too far from home. It was a hideout for many kids of all ages from the surrounding neighborhoods. I always wondered where the creek went and how far it flowed before meeting another body of water or moving out to sea.

On this particular day, before I opened the gate to go into my secret world, I opened the nearby dumpster to throw out some garbage I had brought with me. As I opened the lid, I saw a very dirty naked baby doll in the dumpster. It was one of those simple rubbery baby dolls. I suddenly had a strange urge to save it. Where this came from, I do not know. I was eight years old and a boy. "*Only girls play with dolls,*" I'd often been told. I was going to forget about it and close the dumpster lid, but the desire was too strong. I looked around to make sure I wasn't being watched. I certainly didn't want to be made fun of by any of my friends. As quickly as I could, I took that baby doll out of the dumpster. A part of me knew that it was an odd thing to do and yet I felt I was on an important mission. By now, I had forgotten all about my trip to the creek. Holding that baby doll tightly, I ran home.

I arrived at my empty house. My mother must have been at work and I have no idea where my father and brother were. This was my perfect opportunity to save this baby doll, and I took it. I immediately gave it a bath and wrapped it in a makeshift blanket. I rocked him and let him lie on my bed. *"You'll be safe with me,"* I assured him. *"You are my secret baby and I won't tell anyone about you."*

Although my mother would have been fine with it, I had to keep the baby a secret to keep it safe from everyone else. I felt it was my duty to take care of him. He was clean and safe and I was going to make sure he stayed that way. I knew I had to hide him somewhere so that my brother and father could not find him. I knew if they saw me with a doll, they would make fun of me and call me a sissy and torture me in some way. I quickly made the baby doll a bed in a shoe box, adding some material to keep him comfortable. I put him in the back of the closet. Yes, he would be safe there.

As I went back to my life, there was a sense of power to know I had saved this baby doll and that only I knew about him. It felt powerful to be in control of his safety. After a few days, or it might have been a week, I had to make a new decision. I'd been thinking about it and I knew the baby doll could not remain here with me. I no longer felt he was safe. I was sure he would be found and either be taken away from me or made into a football by my brother. I had to somehow let him go so he could be free of harm.

Because I went to Catholic school, I was familiar with the story of Moses. It was a true story with a happy ending. I decided to create a boat, wrap the baby doll in it, and send him down the creek to a new home where he would be safe. It wasn't the Nile River where Moses was set free but I did hope he would have the same fate.

I remember so clearly the day I decided to let my baby doll go into the turbulent waters to freedom. I knew that my special spot at the creek was the perfect place to let him go. I lined the makeshift shoebox boat with plastic to keep it dry. Making my way to the creek, like a secret agent, I made sure the kids who played at the creek didn't see what I was doing. What would I have told them? I truly didn't understand it myself. What I was doing seemed to go beyond make-believe. My conflicting emotions of sadness and the feeling that I was doing the right thing welled up inside me. I sat with the baby doll for a moment and imagined all the good things that could happen when he was found. As I finally put the boat in the water, I held on tight, not wanting to let go. The waters were flowing and seemed rougher than usual. I held that baby doll and soothed him. *"This is the best thing for you. You'll find a family or a little girl or boy who will take you home just like I did."* I let him know it was too dangerous to stay with me. *"I love you so much. That's why I have to let you go."*

I was finally able to let go of the little boat and off it went. It got caught on some rocks a few feet away from me and I ran down the creek and released it. As I watched my dumpster baby float down the rambling creek, I wondered if he would make it to safety and not tip over and be washed away. I was a good Catholic boy and I knew what to do. I prayed. I'd done my part and I knew that God would handle the rest, just like He did for Moses.

Right now, as a man writing this, I feel a bit embarrassed by this experience. I felt the urge to look up the story of Moses.

"In order to escape death, Moses' mother placed him in

a basket when he was still a baby and set him adrift on the River Nile. She left his fate up to God's will. The infant Moses was rescued by the Pharaoh's daughter and brought up in the palace as a royal prince."

After reading the description of Moses, I am surer than ever that my young knowledge of this story played a role in my mission to free this baby. The question I have is why did an eight-year-old boy go to such great lengths to allow this experience to occur in the first place? As a young child I found incredible coping mechanisms to handle my life amidst the confusion of my father's mental illness. I believe my imagination allowed me to act out what I most likely wanted for myself. It was me I had found on that hot summer day, trapped in a dumpster. The story parallels my out-of-control life. I felt trapped. I felt unsafe. I was saving me on some fantasy level. I was my protector. I wanted to be saved and raised as a prince like Moses. That little boy created a scenario and experience that would assist him in dealing with his fear and give him some peace of mind. I now know that eight-year-old little boy was special and there is nothing to be embarrassed about. I feel a sense of pride for that little boy who reached inside and found a way, although temporary, to cope with his confusing world.

Fulfilling a Promise!

"For every promise, there is a price to pay."

JIM ROHN

Does art imitate life or does life imitate art? I wonder about the answer to this question in regards to how television might affect mental illness. My father watched a lot of TV, including a sitcom from the 1960s called "My Favorite Martian." It was the story of a Martian who came to earth.

> *"Uncle Martin has various unusual powers: He can raise two retractable antennae from the back of his head and become invisible; he is telepathic, and can read and influence minds..."-Wikipedia.org*

While I had my childhood fantasies of being a cowboy, a vampire, or a superhero, my father lived in his own fantasy world. He truly believed that world to be real. He would push and pull those imaginary antennas in and out of his head. He would use them as special communication to aid him in battling his imaginary enemies, or in having desperate conversations with the invisible. If we contradicted him or tried to reason with him, he'd scream and threaten us violently. To him, we were traitors sure to tell the "bad guys" about him. He also used tin foil to cover the windows in the house and in our car and he donned himself with a homemade tin foil hat. Apparently, this behavior is practiced by some who believe in conspiracy theories.

"A tin foil hat is a hat or a piece of conventional headgear lined with foil, often worn in the belief or hope that it shields the brain from threats such as electromagnetic fields, mind control and mind reading. The notion of wearing homemade headgear for such protection has become a popular stereotype and byword for paranoia, persecutory delusions and a belief in pseudoscience and conspiracy theories." - Wikipedia.org

I have always wondered where this mental illness started for my father. Was it nurture, nature, or a deep wound from the traumas of war? My mother told me my father's father kept him in the basement in a cage where he was poked at and tortured. She never gave any more information about his childhood and I don't know how much of this was the truth. However, I did visit my father's childhood home and I was in the presence of his father. I can only say that my deep intuitive feelings informed me that something was not right and I was not safe there.

As I write this, I have such empathy for those who were never quite healed of such traumas and who project those unhealed traumas on their own children. Looking back, I have empathy for both my father and for myself as both of us had to endure the continuance of untreated mental illness. My younger self had an uncanny understanding of my father's pain that allowed me to learn to cope with a childhood that was a shattered photo album. Today, I feel a deep sorrow in my heart for the inner child in many of us, including my father, who have been subjected to mental illness. I feel sorrow for the many inner children who are trapped inside the walls of unresolved conflict.

At the time, I didn't know there were others like our family.

I felt so alone. In my young mind, we were the only ones experiencing such terror and our job was to stay in hiding. I lived two lives. If friends would ask about my father's strange behavior, I would blame it on his drinking. This was understandable because alcohol was common and normal to most everyone. I don't know if they judged us. If they did, it was behind our backs. I didn't think of myself as coping at the time. I was only surviving and continually running from the saber tooth tiger. As the protector of my mother, I survived by learning how to keep my father from harming us which left little time to feel the severity of my situation.

As an older adult asking my little self how I survived in such a frightening environment, I hear this answer, which verifies in my heart what I stated about our experiences in the womb.

"I can't fully remember when I first developed my coping powers, but I believe I started preparing in the womb. My mother was so distressed during her pregnancy with me. I must admit it made me feel like I was somewhat of a burden before I even got here. I think it was because of her secret about me. I was always trying to help her and make her life better. I felt everything that my mother felt when I was in her womb. I even felt her prayers, and she prayed a lot, or should I say begged. She made a lot of promises to God. She even made a bargain with God to not give me dimples or curly hair like my biological father."

When I was twenty-four, the truth about my birth finally came out. My mother let me know that I was the biological son of my father's best army buddy. She let me know that her maid offered to take her to get an abortion. *"I couldn't do it,"* she told me. *"I felt God would punish me and take my other son, Danny, from me."* She refused to abort me although I'm sure it would have been easier for her if I'd never been born.

83

As far as I know, my mother kept her secret well and the father I grew up with (Donovan Engler), who I consider to be my real father, never found out. If he knew, he never let on that he did.

I don't blame my mother for her affair that created me. I'm sure she was making up for my father's lack of attention. The way I look at it is that it brought me here to earth. I'm here and I am grateful for that, even through the turmoil of my childhood.

Back to my mother's prayers while I was in the womb, what she did not realize was that those prayers were being directed to me. This has now been scientifically proven.

> *"The fetus, for example, absorbs excess cortisol and other stress hormones if the mother is chronically anxious. If the child is unwanted for any reason, the fetus is bathed in the chemicals of rejection."* - Dr. Thomas R. Verny, whose pioneering 1981 book, *The Secret Life of the Unborn Child*, first laid out the case for the influence parents have, even in the womb.

And here is more from Dr. Bruce Lipton:

> *"In fact, the great weight of the scientific evidence that has emerged over the last decade demands that we reevaluate the mental and emotional abilities of unborn children. Awake or asleep, the studies show, they (unborn children) are constantly tuned into their mother's every action, thought, and feeling. From the moment of conception, the experience in the womb shapes the brain and lays the groundwork for personality, emotional temperament, and*

the power of higher thought. Up to 50% of a child's personality has already developed by the time of her/his birth. Through the mother's blood that crosses into the placenta, the fetus is learning how to survive in his/her parents' world." -https://www.brucelipton.com/how-much-does-unborn-child-really-know/

I believe I was rearranging my genes to answer her petitions. She was praying to God, and yet what she did not know was that she was talking directly to me. In that moment of her begging and pleading to God, I believe I decided to create this person who would make her life happy and keep her safe. I could make her happy and less anxious. I felt all her feelings, including her fear and guilt. I started my work of serving her before I ever left the womb. It became a mission to make her happy at all costs. Since I was still forming, I was able to straighten my hair and hide my dimples. I would look just like my mother so that no one would ever suspect I wasn't Donovan Engler's son. I think I carried this burden into my life. On some metaphysical level, I had to get here to save and protect her. When I came through the birth canal, I did lose my memory of living that connection with her, but I never seemed to lose the incredible love and the need to prove myself to her. I had to demonstrate that she did not make a mistake by keeping me.

Is it true? Did I make an agreement with my mother before I was fully formed? I find this fascinating and quite exciting. It helps me to understand my deep connection to her and my need to protect her. It is similar to eavesdropping from another room. I'm listening to a conversation she is having, but at the same time, she has no idea I am listening. So, I would spend a lifetime attempting to make her happy. I would not just make up for the pain of having me, but I would even take her childhood sorrows away. I would attempt to make up for all of her emotional pain. My agreement with myself is that I would never become a burden. I would be a good boy to the best of my ability. I would become her savior and then she would have to love me. I would be her Little Man.

Looking back, I can witness that I was quite successful in this mission. However, the question that comes up is, "*At what price?*" Although I never doubted her love for me, I question whether that love was in exchange for my ability to make life easier for her by being the Little Man, as she so fondly called me; a Little Man who was so easily controlled, even into adulthood. Did I unconsciously set a story into motion to be fulfilled by me based on something that happened in the womb? Does it matter? In telling this story, I think it does. It answers many questions about my life today. I cannot redo the past, but I can identify and release the residue of that past that still affects me today.

My mother called me her "Godsend." I never doubted I was just that until her last days when her Godsend disappointed her and did not rearrange his life to continue to prove that he was worth being here. As I will explain later, the day I moved to Kaua'i at fifty-four years old was the day I metaphorically grew up and truly moved out of mother's house.

Back to my original question: "*Little Patrick (Frankie!), How did you cope, handle, and survive such a frightening environment with a mentally ill father?*"

Here is his answer:

> "*I believe I came here equipped to some degree. Everything, including Catholic School, aided me because I believed in something bigger than all the scary stuff going on. The deep love and devotion I had for my mother helped push me through the muck and mire of childhood.*

I survived by praying, crying, and finding the humor in the tragedy. A part of me knew that survival did not depend on what I could do physically. I was just a little boy. It had to depend on what I could do with my mind, my words, and my behavior.

I couldn't attack my father physically. Instead, I used the power of observation. I studied him and learned what made him calm and what escalated him. I got to know his personalities and how they operated. I knew what they were capable of and I knew how to defuse them by using the perfect words."

To this day, I know this is where I learned how to talk someone down from a psychotic moment. I learned that too many words at the wrong moment can be dangerous. I learned the skills of compliments and flattery and I used them to subdue my father. As odd as this metaphor is, I can say I was like a prostitute who knew the seduction of a trick.

I am not sure of the exact age I discovered what my father needed, but I somehow knew his insecurities could become my and my family's security. When he was drunk, I created a space for him to tell me all of his insecurities, and he did. At this time, I call it the *"wife dialogue."* I used it to protect myself from harm. How did I know this dialogue, and what made me instinctively or intuitively know how to execute it? I don't know how I knew. I only know I did.

I knew that my parents did not have an ordinary marriage. My father did not act like the other fathers. My mother treated my father more like a son because he acted like a child. Their yelling matches and his constant insults and name-calling made it clear to me they did not have a romantic relationship. It was also evident to me he didn't feel good about himself. I would try to help, when and if he would listen to me. Although I didn't know the history behind my father's lack of confidence, I intuitively knew he didn't feel capable as a man. If I could give my father what he wanted from my mother, then he would not hurt her or me.

Compulsions, Intuition, and Other Coping Mechanisms

"If the other shoe does drop, I'd rather it lands on joy and gratitude than in a pile of anxiety and fear. Joy is vulnerable."

— Brené Brown

As you can imagine, I lived in a constant state of expectancy, waiting for the next drama. When that first drink was poured, I knew we were in for a ride. A dinner, a picnic, or a graduation could turn into a nightmare. When would the next shoe drop and the nightmare begin?

My brother's high school graduation was one of those times. My father had been drinking, and on the way there, he passed out drunk in the car. We left him there in the car and went into the event. Of course, I couldn't enjoy it. How could I? I was looking over my shoulder the whole time waiting for him to walk in and embarrass everyone. I had plenty of evidence to back up my fear.

That fear turned into a fear of disappointment that would haunt me for many years into adulthood. How many experiences can be ruined by "waiting for the other shoe to drop?" Brené Brown coined the phrase, *"foreboding joy."* This strangling mental habit robs you of the present moment as you consciously prepare yourself for what might happen. Your reasoning is that if you are mentally prepared for doom, it won't hit you as hard when your worst fears come true. Of course, it is one of the biggest lies that we tell ourselves. Now, as an adult, I know we are actually creating our future through what is called "mental rehearsal," using it in a negative sense. However, as a child, it was my shield of protection.

I still made my plans like any kid. I was determined to have friends no matter what. I didn't care if they came to the house only to have to walk over my father passed out on the floor. Even that horrendous Christmas didn't stop me from trying to have a normal childhood. As my father got worse, my mother eventually began to implore me not to bring people to the house. When I was old enough to have the courage to speak up for myself, I'd say, "*You married him, Mom. Not me.*" Yes, I had the courage to say this. Although I took care of my mother and protected her from my father at all costs, I still had a child's longing for friends and community outside of my home. Like all children, I longed for social engagement. This longing soon overcame my desire to be completely subservient to my family. Of course, my actions didn't come without guilt. Also, I'm not saying I wasn't scared of what would happen when those friends came over. I went on, but not without trepidation. My father might have had undiagnosed PTSD, but I had it too. It took the form of hypervigilance. As a child, I literally slept with one eye open. I heard every creak, footstep, and noise. They say that dolphins do this as a form of protecting the pod against predators. My father was definitely a predator to be feared. He might open the door to my room at any time and attack. My eyes were heavy from the bags that formed from lack of sleep. My brother Danny, on the other hand, slept like a log through it all.

I needed relief from living in the war zone called my family. We were driven out of the house in the middle of the night, in constant fear of violence. Would one of my father's personalities come out to end our lives? When would the next screaming and raging begin? My father's illusionary world was thrust upon us. We all lived at war with his mental illness. I navigated this war by becoming a child mediator, learning how to manipulate my father to keep us safe and protecting our secret from the outside world by fabricating stories to tell the neighbors.

There were times that my father in his delusionary state would stand behind our trailer and throw eggs over the roof at other people's homes. He thought they were grenades. Of course, the neighbors were not happy to have their houses egged and I was the one they blamed. They called my mother, but in her embarrassment about my father, she didn't know exactly how to handle it. I stepped in without being asked. "*I'll handle it*," I told her. I approached the neighbors to let them know it wasn't me and my father had been the egg thrower. I made excuses. "*The reason my dad egged your house was because he sometimes has bad memories about the war.*" They accepted my explanation. They'd already seen and heard enough coming from our home. How did I know to say this when no one told me? It seemed I had a psychology degree at an early age. It was a coping mechanism that kept me and the family safe. It also kept our family secret safe. As a child, I was forced to become a mental health expert in order to survive. Later, I would pay thousands of dollars to receive a diploma in psychology.

A story that illustrates my role as therapist, confidant, counselor, and Little Man to my mother was when I was around seven and we were still living on Clinton Avenue. We had a traditional Toll House Chocolate Chip Cookie night every Tuesday. Perhaps some of you reading this remember those cookies, especially the cookie dough. My brother especially loved the chocolate chips and his love for those chips would turn what should have been a warm Hallmark night into a horror show instead. My mother always made an effort at normalcy and Toll House Cookie nights were one of those attempts. Like clockwork, right after the dishes were done and my mother began the weekly baking night, we'd here a scream from the kitchen, "*DANNY! DANNY! Get in this kitchen now!*"

Waving the ripped empty bag in her hand with her eyes ready to pop, she'd scream, "*Danny, did you eat the chocolate chips? Did you?*"

Why she asked every week, I never knew. The answer was always the same. With a sheepish grin covering up a devious smile, Danny would deny a couple of rounds of her asking until she'd finally explode with, "*Why, Danny? Why? You know that we make cookies on Tuesdays. Why, Danny, why?*"

"*I don't know Mom. I don't know,*" he would say, crying. He knew what was coming.

She would either slap him or hold him by the shoulders, forcing him to look her in the face as she implored over and over, "*Why, why, why?*" Finally, he'd be sent to his room.

After these weekly episodes, I would ask Danny why he did this when he knew how Mom was going to react. "*Ah, you just enjoy watching me get punished,*" was his answer.

He didn't understand that I hated it and it was torture for me. Sadly, I began to hate and dread Toll House cookie nights. This scene went on repeatedly for more Tuesdays than I care to remember. With sobs, I'd ask my mother, "*Why do you keep buying the chocolate chips? Please stop buying them, Mom. I hate this. The cookies aren't important to me and Danny's never going to stop eating them. Wouldn't it be easier not to buy the chocolate chips?"*

One night, she finally got it. I could feel a sense of calm from her. Solemnly, she just said, *"You're right Frankie. I'll stop buying them. It's not worth it."*

She wiped my tears away and hugged me. *"Thank you, Mom. Thank you so much."*

My mother listened to me. I was seven years old and she took my advice. I was really happy that my brother would not be punished on Toll House Tuesday Nights. I don't think he ever knew about that white flag I waved at my mother in order to end the cookie war on Clinton Avenue in Richmond, California.

As I said, I had a lot of compulsions and coping skills that allowed me to control my life in some bizarre way. I had a compulsion to clean. I organized the cupboards and alphabetized the cans, cleaned the oven, did the wash, cleaned the windows, vacuumed incessantly, ironed, and beat the dust from the furniture. I was a prep cook for my mother. When she arrived home from work at 5:30 p.m., I prided myself on having all the ingredients, peeled potatoes or whatever else was needed, ready for her to cook. I frequently washed all the ashtrays in the house. Unfortunately for my father, I would leave a wet film that would inevitably put out his cigarettes. I didn't do it on purpose and I didn't care if he yelled about it. It didn't stop me from cleaning those ashtrays and everything else in the house.

My compulsion to control my environment led to list-making in every moment. I scheduled my days in hopes of gaining order in my life. This obsessive behavior actually calmed me and gave me a sense of power. I knew it most definitely pleased my mother and I liked that. She thanked me for allowing her to come home to a clean house. Her positive feedback made me feel strong. When I was in ninth grade, I received an allowance for my compulsions. I even started my own cleaning business in high school. No one found my behavior odd or thought to ask me why. My brother and father used it as another reason to call me a sissy, a little girl. Could their incessant teasing be their way of alleviating their guilt, especially when my mother admonished them about not doing anything to help while she was out earning a living for the family? I think I am making excuses for their bad behavior. Guilt didn't seem to be anything close to what I experienced from my father and Danny.

Today, I am a man known for his humor. As I look back, I know my ability to find humor in my life was most definitely another coping mechanism that started in my childhood. I developed characters and even mimicked my father's outrageous behavior in skit-like fashion. I learned that laughter made people feel better. When I imitated my father, it would make my mother laugh. I had already given my mother martyr status and to see her laugh felt good to me. The only person who didn't think I was funny was my brother. *"You're a show-off!"* he'd sneer. *"You just want people's attention."*

I cried a lot too, but mostly when I was alone. I had my share of reasons and I allowed myself to shed plenty of tears. I believe that allowing myself to cry was a positive coping mechanism. Releasing my emotions gave me the strength to meet the next family drama.

Eventually, when my father's mental illness was diagnosed, medications entered the play of our lives and they gave him some relief. This relief, of course, trickled down to all of us. One question I still ponder is the difference between my brother and me. We lived in the same household, and yet he went on to self-destruction while I craved a better life. I remember my mother on her many attempts to leave my father. My brother and I had an army counselor talk to us for a moment. "*How do you feel about your parents divorcing?*" he'd ask. "*Do you feel guilty or that it's your fault?*"

Danny always expressed his rage about my parents divorcing. My answer was simple, "*I did not marry my father. My mother did and that was their marriage. How could I be to blame?*"

I would beg my mother to get a divorce and my brother begged her to stay with him. At one point, she almost did get divorced. I was elated but my brother begged her not to. At the last minute at the courthouse, she changed her mind. I remember the feeling of doom and of being alone in my feelings. It was as though the jail doors opened and then were suddenly closed on us again. Would we ever leave this prison?

I remember drawing stick figures to represent my family unit. I had my mother in the middle holding up my brother on one shoulder and my father on the other. I drew myself, the Little Man, under my mother, holding them all on my shoulders. I drew this picture twice; once when I was little and once in a psychology class in college. I can remember the professor in my psychology class asking to see me. I was eighteen years old at the time. She sat with me and talked to me about why I drew it. I can't remember the whole conversation but I know it gave me a feeling of peace to finally let my secret out to someone else.

Later in life, I showed my mother the picture and she said she completely understood. At different times, she would bring up that picture when trying to explain our relationship to other people. It seemed that she was proud of me and didn't think of it as unhealthy. I wonder about that. Maybe having someone love her that much made her feel worthy. My pain was not her journey nor anything we ever spoke about. It would take me going into therapy to work out the dysfunction of my childhood and many years of spiritual work to realize how healthy I really was.

My Therapy Comes Through TV

"Why let go of yesterday? Because yesterday has already let go of you."

- STEVE MARABOLI

On those afternoons when my mother was still at work, I was sometimes greeted by a father who wasn't a terror. I loved to watch afternoon TV with him. He turned me on to the show *Dark Shadows*, a great soap opera. I continued to watch that show for many years. Before *Dark Shadows* aired, there was another show that might have been labeled my therapy. It increased my understanding of what I was going through in real life. It was another soap opera called *One Life to Live*. Like all good soap operas, if you watch more than five minutes of it, you will get hooked. *One Life to Live* was no different, especially for a little boy who hungered for escape. My father didn't care and my mother wasn't home. I look at it now from a distance and think how unlike the other little boys I really was. The show contained such adult material but I seemed to understand it. I guess being labeled the Little Man was not too far from the truth.

More importantly, there was a certain character on *One Life to Live* who helped me to normalize my life with my father, the Dr. Jekyll and Mr. Hyde of my childhood. This character most definitely allowed me to give my father's mental illness some kind of a meaning. The character was

Victoria Lord, the rich daughter of Victor Lord. It was Victoria's wedding day and she was about to marry Joe Riley, a newspaper reporter, totally against her "Big Daddy" Victor Lord's wishes. Just as she is about to say, "*I do,*" she stops and starts to rub her head as though she has a horrible headache. As she does, she takes on a totally different personality — Nicki Smith. Nicki is bold and full of spunk, unlike the refined Victoria. With a totally different voice, Nicki grabs Vinnie Wolak, Joe Riley's best friend, and says, "*Come on baby. Let's get out of this joint.*" Just like that, they run off from the wedding.

Witnessing Victoria Lord helped me to know there were people like my father. I wasn't alone. She behaved just as I had watched my father act when a whole new person emerged from him. The characters in the show dealt with Vicky's multiple personalities and her psychiatrist gave theories and diagnosis to her and the family. I felt like I had some kind of understanding of my father. Although my own father was not diagnosed fully with paranoid schizophrenia until much later, as I went through the journey with Victoria, some part of my imaginative faculties was normalizing my father. I knew they were actors, and yet it helped me to understand my father a little more. It amazes me that my younger self took opportunities with characters on TV to process and attempt to understand my father.

On those afternoons, I felt I wanted to be an actor and play roles that were fun. My TV watching didn't stop there. There was *Peyton Place*, the scandalous nighttime soap opera. Children were not allowed to watch it, especially if you went to Catholic School. It dealt with otherwise unspeakable subjects like rape, murder, incest, abortion, promiscuity, and adultery. It first aired in 1964. I was only six years old. The cast was comprised of future stars: Mia Farrow, Ryan O'Neal,

Barbara Perkins, and Leslie Nelson, just to name a few.

I didn't sleep much at night. I remember sneaking up behind my mother as she watched the show. She'd try to ignore me, then finally motioned to me to sit next to her. On this particular night, my father wasn't there. Perhaps he was off on some job or in the hospital recovering from another episode. I can still recall a character named Ann White who fell off a cliff to her death. She had just found out that the man she was dating was her brother, so they were not sure if it was murder or suicide. I was crying when they found her dead. My mother comforted me of six or seven understanding that subject matter.

The following day I was still broken-hearted about the death of Ann White and I shared it with a friend of mine, Trisha. She told her mother and her mother told Sister Mary Elva. I was called to Sister Mary Elva's office. If I had known I was going to get my mother and me in trouble, I would never have said a word. I didn't know that, so when asked if I watched *Peyton Place*, I confirmed it, "*Yes, I did watch the show.*" She called my mother right away telling her it was inappropriate for me to watch such a scandalous show. Our life was secret and now I had let a secret out into the world. I was sure I would get it when I got home, but instead my mother responded both to Sister Mary Elva and Trish's mother. To Sister Mary Elva she said, "*You are only responsible for my son between the hours of 8:00 a.m. and 3:00 p.m. I'll make decisions about him after that.*"

Then, my mother let Trish's mother know, "*What happens in our home and what we watch on TV is none of your business.*"

Unfortunately, after that, Trish's mother wouldn't let me play with her anymore. I told my mother I was sorry.

"Frankie," she said, *"Don't tell people things they won't understand."*

She wasn't mad but the message was clear. We needed to be more careful with the outside world. It was a challenge because I did like to talk. Now, I had to constantly monitor what I said. I still struggle with this to this day. You see, I am a transparent person and I do my best to remain authentic. It is definitely not something I would change about myself. A lot can be said about my mother and how she handled my father and our situation, but I was always proud of how she held her own and defended us from what she called "busybodies." I remember when I was an altar boy. One of the ladies in the church told her I giggled during service. My mother's retort was, *"If you'd been busy praying like you should have been, maybe you wouldn't have noticed what my son was or wasn't doing."*

So, *Peyton Place* allowed me to see and listen to other dysfunctional families and relationships and let me know that I was not alone. Similarly, *One Life to Live* taught me about multiple personalities and helped me understand and somewhat normalize my father and his mental illness.

Aristotle, echoed by St Ignatius Loyola said, *"Give me a child till he is seven years old, and I will show you the man."*

That tells me a lot about this Little Man of seven. On some level, I feel like I was always more of an adult. As I write this, I am not sure if I believe it was wrong to allow me to watch those shows. I do appreciate *One Life to Live* and *Peyton Place* for educating me on some very difficult periods of my life. I believe I was always being guided. Guidance can come in many forms, even in the shape of scandalous soap operas. I know that no matter how it affected me, I must choose gratitude or I will be stuck in the past forever. My choice is to bless the past and not curse it. As Steve Maraboli wrote, *"Let go of the past because the past has already let go of you."*

Why Did She Stay?

"Maturity, one discovers, has everything to do with the acceptance of 'not knowing'."
- MARK Z. DANIELEWSKI

The question as to why my mother stayed with my father when he was dangerous to all of us comes up quite a bit when I speak about my early life. From a logical viewpoint, she was the one who put us in danger by staying in her marriage and in the abuse inflicted on all of us by my father. I can feel myself saying, *"Stop! Can I say that? Is she watching me as I write these words?"* Yes, I can feel myself wanting to protect my mother so that people will not think badly of her. Truly, as a child, I felt my mother was a saint; a real Joan of Arc.

My first answer to this question of why my mother stayed in this frightening relationship is, *"I do not truly know."* Anything I could say would only be me psychoanalyzing her or guessing. Does anyone really know why some people do what they do? Until we walk in another person's shoes, we are merely speculating. Even when we do share the same experience as another person, we still don't know what's really in their minds. I have come to understand that everything in life is ruled by our perception without any knowledge of what another person is really going through.

Through the years I asked my mother a lot of questions, and for the most part, she answered them as truthfully as she could. She probably shared more than she should with a son. Although I never got the answer to this question fully, I surmised that my mother was really not just our protector, but my father's protector as well. Behind all his emerging personalities, my mother protected the good, the bad, and the ugly of my father. As I think about the whole situation now, I realize if it hadn't been for my mother, my father would more than likely have been one of those homeless people who roam the streets suffering with mental illness without any help at all. I feel I got through a very turbulent childhood with my father because my mother was there for me. That might seem strange given the circumstances of my childhood, but I know she protected me to the best of her ability, sometimes even putting herself in danger. Later, in conversation and maybe in defense of her actions, she would always say, "*I never let him hurt you.*"

My mother prided herself on never letting my father hit me or my brother. When he would go after us, she would stand in front of him, blocking us from his blow. Yet, she wasn't always there for us. How could she be? I remember my brother getting yanked out of our bunk bed by my father in the middle of the night right after having a tonsillectomy. There were many scenes like that one. There is also a psychological fear of being hit, yelled at, yanked out of bed in the middle of the night, or waiting for your mother to scream. As I said, I slept with one eye open and every creak, footstep, breath, or just the house breathing its natural sounds were amplified in my mind. At the time, I think my mother really felt satisfaction in thinking she never let my father hurt us on a physical level. Yet she did not realize the internal pain we experienced. Many in my mother's generation didn't think beyond the present moment. Therapy was not something in which they engaged. It would have been considered "*airing the family's dirty laundry.*" You just don't do that. It wasn't until her elderly years that she even mentioned how she realized how damaging life with my father must have been for my brother and me. In her own understanding, she realized my childhood was shortchanged, but not to the level that I understood what really happened to me. I couldn't explain to her that the constant worry for her safety and my looking for ways to make her happy (to make up for the life she did not have with my father) was what constituted that shortchanged childhood. I couldn't explain to her what I had learned through therapy; that I was my father's surrogate wife and my mother's surrogate husband. I believe my mother went to her grave without processing much of the drama we experienced.

As I write this story, I notice I do not use the word abuse very often. However, mental illness, alcoholism, and dysfunction are used frequently. The little boy inside me knows differently. "*We were abused.*" I am not afraid to admit it because it has led to my healing.

In spite of all this, my mother and I were very close throughout my life. I became her confidant at a young age and never quite gave up that role. She even shared many of her stories and feelings about the life she had with my father before I was born; how easy it was for her to express many of her deepest feelings with me. As I look back now, it made the Little Man feel important to take on such a role. It gave my mother an emotional intimacy she was not getting from her husband. I gave my mother a rest from the constant turmoil my father created. I had a goal that stopped me from running away from home. My sole purpose was to make her happy, no matter what.

Later, as a man, I found ways to make up for her childhood pain of growing up without a father. Her father (my grandfather) died when she was two years old. He was quite the name in Kansas City and left my grandmother with five kids to raise. They were left with a considerable fortune but the money was squandered by relatives, and soon my mother and her family were penniless.

As an adult at Christmas, I made sure my mother had a tree full of presents to make up for the years of poverty she experienced. It became a way of life for me. It never felt unnatural and I would probably do it again. I'm not saying it was a healthy relationship for a son to have with his mother but I spent many years unconscious of that.

And so, I buried the question of why my mother stayed with my father with my adoration for her. When I went through puberty and started to grow up and gain some of my own thoughts and perceptions, I began to ask the question more deeply. I became cognizant of how wrong it was for my father to torture his family. Why would she subject herself and her children to this nightmare? However, she was my role model and I adored her. I thought of her as strong, not a victim of my father's abuse. I blamed him for the disruption in our family. It never dawned on me my mother had a choice in all this madness.

Instead, I used my humor to make her laugh. I innately knew that humor and laughter made people feel better and forget for a moment about their pain or fear. I was my mother's personal standup comedian and once again I felt important. Even as an adult, I continued to imitate my father, his dialogue, the scenes that tortured our lives, and somehow this lessened the severity of what had really gone on. It was a coping strategy even in adulthood. When I'd see my mother smile or laugh at my crazy antics, it gave me a sense of control of her feelings and my own.

As I continue to disclose the dysfunctional events and experiences, I feel a lot of different emotions. Although

I have addressed these memories of my father and all the experiences of pure terror, I can be one step away from still activating the fear in my body as though it were happening in the present moment. The scientist, teacher, and author, Dr. Joe Dispenza, says healing takes place when we can remember the event without the emotional tie to it. I feel I am finally able to do that. As I write this, I marvel at my little boy who is still there protecting his mommy and feels he is going to get into trouble if he says anything that makes her look bad. I am taking a moment to assure that brave little boy that he will not get in trouble.

If my mother were here now, I would tell her I have an opportunity to help others on their journey through mental illness or alcoholism. I have the opportunity to help women or men in a similar situation to get help or even make better choices. If I asked her permission, I hope she would understand. However, I tell my little boy I cannot guarantee that she would agree with me writing this book. It is a decision that I, as an adult, have to make alone. I do not believe my mother was a "bad mother." She did the best she could with what she knew at the time. But I do believe that her choices affected me and my brother. We all suffered from the choices she made and I am sure she suffered to a large degree knowing she did that to us. I am not wanting my mother to suffer. We all did enough of that. This book is about love, forgiveness, and letting go.

In order to let go, we have to face what happened and how we feel about it first. I don't think we ever want to blame our parents as much as we want to understand the events that happened. One thing I have never blamed myself for was my father and his behavior. I was clear at an early age that although I was in this family, the responsibility was with them, not me. At one of those times when I went to the army doctor for one of my stomachaches, I remember the doctor asked me if I blamed myself for any of the trouble my parents were having. Blaming myself was not the case, and I let that doctor know, just as I had let that therapist know, *"She married him. I didn't!"* On the other hand, my brother did blame himself. He wanted a father no matter how it was packaged. I believe this led to a lot of my brother's future problems and final demise.

I remember asking my mother why she married my father. Her answer was, to get out of Kansas City and see the world. He was in the army and that enabled her to travel wherever he was stationed. What a crazy way to see the world! Many people do not truly think their decisions through. My mother was one of those people. She also confided in me that her self-esteem was always in question. When she married my father, he would never touch her sexually. Alcohol was always a constant bed partner in their marriage. She blamed the bottle but still confided that she always wondered what was wrong with her. I believe it weighed heavily on her and how she valued herself. Perhaps that accounted for her many affairs.

There were so many contradictions in my parents' married life that add confusion to the question of my mother staying with my father. For example, my parents were members of the Moose Lodge. Drinking was an accepted activity there and my father was not the only person making a scene. He had plenty drinkers to join him. The difference was that he became uncontrollable. I was not allowed in the Moose Lodge after 9:00 p.m., but I had plenty of experiences with him at the fish fries, birthday steak dinners, and the Moose Lodge family Sunday barbeques. I must say, one never knew what my father was going to do at these events. My mother knew this but continued to encourage him to come.

She would even bring him to her work picnics. This was surprising since she lived in fear of him embarrassing her. How could she not know it would be no different at her work place? However, in spite of his past behavior, she would give it a chance, and as always, we had to leave the picnic early before he would make a scene. I prayed constantly that one day I wouldn't care anymore about the embarrassment that my father brought to my life. It never happened.

When my father was drunk, he sometimes talked of suicide. My mother never seemed to take him seriously because he had said it for so many years. He was always threatening to jump off the Golden Gate Bridge. My mother's reply was, "*Would you like me to drive you?*" I knew she wasn't serious about driving him to the bridge. It was all part of the dysfunction. My father never attempted suicide. Perhaps his talk of suicide was his way of trying to kill off that demon part of himself. We were not trained for these mental disorders. How did I handle it? When he would talk to me about suicide, I would tell him what I thought he wanted to hear. "*Don't Dad. I love you!*"

Why did my mother stay with my father? There are many reasons I could give you, like she was a product of the culture and the time period, or as a Catholic woman in the1960s, divorce was to be avoided at all costs. However, does it matter? Will it change anything? I think what matters is that she did stay with him and we did suffer a life with my father's dis-ease. Although, I have continued to be confused by all of my mother's contradictions in her relationship with my father, I have stopped trying to figure it out. It's relieved me of any attachment I have trying to make my past different.

The real question is: how did I survive and thrive in spite of it? Bob Proctor, a self-help master, states in many of his presentations, "*There is good in everything.*" Is that a

Pollyanna attitude? Is that a cop out in my case? I don't think so because there was good. I grew older and faced it all. I chose to find that good. It was part of my healing to know that what has already happened cannot be changed. It is only our perception of it that can be changed.

Broken Promises

"Forgiveness is the answer to the child's dream of a miracle by which what is broken is made whole again, what is soiled is made clean again."

— DAG HAMMARSKJOLD

As I write this book, I received an invite to my fifty-year grade school/middle school class reunion. I graduated from St. David's Catholic School in 1972. Although I began at St. David's in the second grade, I still had seven years with this class, progressing from childhood through puberty. This was my family away from home. All those years at St. David's took place during the peak of my father's mental illness.

It's truly unbelievable that fifty years have passed. The reunion gives me a sense of excitement, sadness, and uncomfortableness. These feelings stem from the anticipation of being reunited with my past. As the planning of the reunion is in motion, the organizer is sending photos and the names of the attendees as well as the names of those who have passed away. I am finding many memories are surfacing when certain names are mentioned. Leslie was one of those names. She was the very first girl I asked out on a date. We were in the seventh grade. My feelings can only be described as both awkward and magical. It might seem that the details of this part of my life are unimportant, but while thinking of Leslie, I am remembering another relationship – the one I had with my mother.

Leslie and I met for our first date at Pub Hut Hot Dog

Restaurant in Richmond. Her mother dropped her off. I got there on my own. We spent time eating our hotdogs and talking. Our feelings for each other were mutual. I liked her and she liked me. The feeling was exciting. I was focused on a girl other than my mother. I remember one night when we were all at my friend Denise's house. We were playing the game Truth or Dare. When it was my turn, my question was directed to Leslie. I wrote on a piece of paper, "*Will you go steady with me?*" This was a huge moment in a young boy's life. Would she reject me? She was excited and screamed with joy, "*Yes, I will go steady with you.*" I remember Leslie and Denise both dancing and jumping up and down.

After we parted that evening, Leslie gave me a hug. I watched her and Denise walking down the street, giggling. I could hear Leslie's voice. She was excited and elated. "*I can't believe he asked me to go steady.*" I should have been excited too, but a sinking feeling came over me. I had the oddest thought that seemed to come out of nowhere. "*What have I done? I can't go steady. What about Mom?*"

Strangely, as I write this, this foreboding feeling feels fresh and new. I knew that I couldn't do this to my mother. I was her protector. My father was getting worse. She needed me. I had no time to be going steady with anyone. As I look back on this, I am aware of how crazy this was. In that moment, my mother didn't even know. I had no legitimate reason for my feelings besides a young boy's deep feelings of being the protector of his family with no room for any other relationships.

Leslie called me that same night. She was excited and just wanted to talk. "*I'm sorry,*" I choked on the words. "*I made a mistake. I can't go steady with you.*" I broke a young girl's heart in that moment, but mine was broken too. Leslie and I were never the same after that. I remember seeing her in high school and still she gave me the cold shoulder.

As I get ready for this reunion, I wonder if she still carried this hurt after all these years. I would never find out because I was told she passed away. When I found out that she had died, I felt such sadness. I wanted to make it right and tell her the real reason I deserted her. If I could tell her now I would say, "*Leslie, I wish I had told you the silly reason why I called us off that day. I wished I had told you I didn't feel like I had a choice. I had to take care of my mother. I loved our date at the Pub Hut Hot Dog Restaurant and I really wanted to go steady with you. That is the truth! I am sorry for any pain that I caused you in one of the most important times in your development. Rest in Power, my first girlfriend.*"

I am so grateful to come to this closure, to understand the little mind that was so indebted to the protection of his family that he even gave up a part of himself and his development. Having this clarity now is healing. I look forward to this reunion and the other memories it will bring forward for healing.

***

I did attend the fifty-year reunion. Surprisingly, it wasn't healing in and of itself, but allowed me to realize I have already healed. It became an interesting and fun experience to connect with so many memories and people I knew back then. The reunion was only one evening and I wished it had been longer. We had some great conversations, some laughs, and some processing of the school dramas that we experienced in Catholic school back in the 1960s.

My wife and I spent time touring many of the featured areas of my childhood. Very little of the locations were left. St. David's was still there and I was happy to have the opportunity to roam its halls. There was one significant place still remaining and that was Clinton Avenue. When my wife and I pulled up in front of that house, it seemed so small compared to all that went on there. A woman came out of the house next door. I could tell she was a little nervous, perhaps wondering who we were and why we were parked in front of the house. When I rolled down my window and explained, she got really friendly and she said, "*I have to call my mom. I think she knew your family.*"

She got her mother on the phone and handed it to me. That woman most definitely remembered my family. However, in our conversation, she didn't mention any of the drama that I have explained in this book. I don't know if she was being polite or if perhaps in her old age, she had forgotten. How did I feel talking to her? I have to be honest. My feelings of being embarrassed about my father's behavior were still there, but not enough to bring up a strong emotion.

What did I learn from a physical trip back into my past? All in all, I was glad I went to the reunion. Through the conversations I engaged in with different people along the way, I came to realize that so many of the things I remembered with such ferocity and emotion and yes, sometimes embarrassment, had long been forgotten by others. My journey to those familiar places helped me to realize that although it was my past, my history, it was over and it was time to truly move on.

A Graduation Present from Sister Margaret Marie

"Hurtful words are deep cuts in the heart. They may heal over time, but the scars never completely disappear."

- ANOIR OU-CHAD

Graduation from St. David's Elementary was just a few weeks away and the feeling of freedom was in the air. Everyone felt it, but there was also a sadness to it. We were like a family. We had been together for eight years, traveling from class to class every day. Naturally a few would leave and others would join us over the years, but the initial feeling of family never left us. Now as we made our way to graduation day, we would enter different high schools. The family would separate. We knew it would never be the same again.

Before that final graduation day, I was called to Principal Sister Margaret Marie's office. Being summoned to her office was not a usual occurrence, but little did I know, she would give me a graduation gift I would carry with me for a great portion of my life. As I walked slowly to Sister Margaret Marie's office, I remembered that she'd recently gotten really sick. They told us she had a stroke and she had to stop teaching. I hadn't seen her for a while, and when I was told she wanted to see me, I felt paralyzed. I'd never been in a convent. As I write this, I can only describe it as walking into a haunted house.

I couldn't imagine what she would want to say to me but my intuition told me it was not good. My memories of my time at St. David's flooded into my mind. Our class already had a reputation as troublemakers, but I never thought of us as that. We were just a group of kids who tried to change the rules and advance things. For example, we asked for the first girl/boy party in seventh grade. Our parents supported it and we got it. We were all for having fun and making what we considered to be positive changes. We all knew we were not really liked as a class and I was considered to be the ringleader. As Sister Margaret Marie and other teachers would inform my mother at parent-teacher meetings, "*He's not a bad kid or directly disobedient. It's just when he talks, the children laugh, listen, and act like he's a king.*"

My mother asked logical questions about my behavior, but all she got back from Sister Margaret Marie was that the kids thought I was king and she lost control of the class due to my presence. I did get in trouble a lot for talking. To no avail, as the years went by, I was moved around from desk to desk to see if there was a place I would not talk. They even tried surrounding me with non-talkers and smart kids. It never worked. I enticed everyone into conversation with me and I spent many times at the blackboard writing, "I SHALL NOT TALK IN CLASS," over and over until it filled the board.

They say affirmations work, but you have to believe them. I didn't believe I was a non-talker. I liked to talk. Now, I wasn't interrupting the teacher. I was just doing what I considered to be commentary on what was being said. Sometimes, I would raise my hand excessively, asking questions or answering them even when I didn't know the answer.

My father was most definitely crazed by my talking. I remember him screaming, *"Do you ever shut the fuck up???"*

Thinking a little deeper on this point, I realize that my incessant talking came from my need to be heard. Was anyone really listening to me? I also think that perhaps talking allowed me to divert others from asking me questions that might force me to reveal what was really happening in my life. Perhaps if I kept the conversation going in other directions, my family secret would never be found out. One thing I do know that made my teachers mad was my ability to make my fellow students laugh. I wasn't trying to be funny but they really found me humorous. Laughing in a strict environment like St. David's was definitely frowned upon.

Back to my graduation and my summons to Sister Margaret Marie's office in 1972, I wondered if this could be about an incident where I defended a fellow classmate who was being humiliated by a teacher. Mr. Thomas, a part-time social studies teacher, had disciplined one of my fellow students by taking the garbage can filled with milk cartons and leftovers from lunch and placing it on the boy's head. The student had to sit in the corner while Mr. Thomas went on with the class as if nothing had happened. I couldn't take my eyes off the milk dripping onto this poor boy's head and body. I was astonished he didn't even fight it. He just sat there. Everyone was frozen with terror. I couldn't stand it. I had to do something but I was as scared as everyone else. Mr. Thomas noticed my reaction, stopped, and called on me, *"You have a problem?"* he snarled, daring me to speak.

"Yes, I do." My voice quivered, but I kept going, *"It is not right or fair to do that to him. It is wrong."*

You could hear a pin drop. *"Get up here!"* roared Mr. Thomas.

I walked slowly to the front of the room. Mr. Thomas walked over to the boy and removed the garbage can from his head. Stuff fell all over the floor. He stood staring at me, holding the can. "*You don't think it is fair, huh?*" Mr. Thomas grabbed me and started to shove the can over my head. "*No, No, No!*" I screamed, as I held my hands tightly on the can to stop him.

I still wonder how the other kids could just sit there. The door suddenly flung open and a nun who was acting as principal came in. I thought she was coming to save me. "*What is going on? What are you doing?*" she yelled. To my surprise, she wasn't shouting at Mr. Thomas. She was yelling at me! I started to explain what happened but she abruptly grabbed me by the hand. I thought I was being rescued, but she had other plans. "*Be quiet and come with me!*" she screamed and yanked me out of the room.

My mother was not happy about being called away from her job. The message was clear. "*Why do you have to cause trouble?*" I thought I'd done something good. I spoke up for what was right, but I was being punished while Mr. Thomas's behavior was ignored. I was on trial once again for being a troublemaker. I remember being the only one who stood up to Mr. Thomas. Everyone else sat at their desks, terrified. I was left alone and it was never spoken about again. "*Don't talk about it*" was a theme in my life. I had the opportunity to see that boy at the fifty-year reunion. He hardly remembered the incident but it was the story most talked about by everyone else.

As I walked to Sister Margaret Marie's office that day, I wondered if this incident would finally come up. I fantasized that maybe she would tell me that she really did think I was a good kid. I walked very slowly, with my heart beating, as I made up possible scenarios. I rang the doorbell. It took a moment and the housekeeper opened the door and told me to follow her. The house was dark and I could see the little chapel with the stained-glass windows and statues all through the corridors. I felt like I was in a scary movie. However, although I was frightened, there was a part of me that felt somewhat special and excited. After all, I was seeing a place that very few people are allowed to see or experience. *"This is where they go when they are not with us,"* I thought. It was lonely in a strange way and so very quiet. The housekeeper brought me to a small room with a few chairs and a desk. The scene played out in slow motion as I waited for Sister Margaret Marie's arrival. After what seemed like forever, she entered and I stood and greeted her as we always did, *"Good afternoon, Sister Margaret Marie."*

With a steely-eyed expression and a stern voice, she simply said, *"Sit down!"*

She had a look of complete disgust on her face. She looked so angry. I tried to speak, *"How are you feeling, Sis…"*

She cut me off. *"Don't!"*

I knew my only job was to listen. My ears couldn't believe what they were hearing. *"I have never been so happy in all my teaching history to see a class graduate and leave this school. You and your whole class are why I had this stroke. Grief and stress, that's what you've caused me."*

I tried to stand up for myself. *"I don't understand how this can be my fault."*

"You are a leader. They look up to you. They treat you like you are a king. And you think you are so funny. They all laugh."

"I'm sorry," I tried to apologize. *"It was never my intention to hurt you or disrupt the school."*

Her face was getting very red. I hoped she didn't have another stroke. *"Just get out — and get out of my school too!"*

That's all I remember. I forgot how I left or if we ever talked again. I only recall her disgust for me. So, that was my graduation present from Sister Margaret Marie. I wonder how much of that gift I still have in the recesses of my mind. I don't remember ever telling my mother. I didn't want to hear her theory of "not rocking the boat."

And right now, as I write this, I am still in shock about how someone who calls herself "spiritual" could feel such an intense hatred for a child. Perhaps it stemmed from her own unhappiness. I guess I'll never know. The question for me is: How many boats have I not rocked because of her judgment? I will say that when I look back on my life, I have been a boat-rocker in spite of the memory of this dramatic story. My subconscious fear of causing trouble is outweighed by a stronger conscious conviction to do what is necessary and right.

Was There Anything Good About My Father?

> *"Be happy not because everything is good, but because you can see the good side of everything."*
> - DALE PARTRIDGE

Without turning my father into a victim or a martyr because of his conditions, I must remember that his own dysfunctional family and the atrocities of war played a huge part in who he became. However, was there anything good about him? This is a question frequently asked of me by those knowing some of my history. We did have some good times and they are worth mentioning so as to see that beneath and beyond the mental disease, a true good soul still lived. I feel that my father is worthy of a chapter, a spotlight, focusing on the good he brought to the family and to me.

The real truth is I had more than one father. Think of Dr. Jekyll and Mr. Hyde. When he drank his potion, in this case alcohol, the nightmare began. However, there was a peaceful, fun, and almost normal father at other times. Drunk or sober, my father would give you the shirt off his back until Mr. Hyde (his mean personality) would fully take over. My mother was wary of his generosity as the family was sure to suffer financially as a result. Sometimes, it took the form of him giving his entire paycheck away to strangers. Of course,

I didn't mind that generosity when it meant extra cash in my piggy bank.

I remember Crab Saturdays. My parents loved crab and it was a special treat because funds were so low. My father would bring that crab home, put it on the bar with the hammer for cracking, and the beer would follow. He would always offer me some crab and my mother's eyes told me to refuse. It was too expensive to waste on me as I did not care that much for crab. However, as far as my father was concerned when it came to food, we all should eat the same. If there were rare treats like crab, it was for all of us. At some of my friend's' houses, on steak nights the kids were given hotdogs or hamburgers. When I told my father this, he would say, "*We all eat the same thing. If we can't all have steaks, nobody has steaks. And no catsup on the steaks! It ruins the taste of an expensive meal.*" How easily we are programed in our formative years. To this day, when I see someone put catsup or steak sauce on steak, I freeze and expect my parents to stop them.

Dinner was always served at 6:00 p.m. during the work week. Even if my father was passed out in his mashed potatoes, the four of us would sit at that table. It was important to my mother to keep some normalcy even during the chaos. When my father was himself, we would have general conversations about our day. I remember in the mobile home there was a long mirror over the wooden counters. As I would eat or talk, I would look at myself in that mirror. I seemed to be observing myself in my environment and was fascinated with how I looked as I was interacting at the table. My brother would yell to my mother, "*Mom, he won't stop looking at himself. Tell him to stop it!*" To this day I wonder why it bothered him so much. It always caused an argument between us until my mother or father would stop it. I think it was probably my inner actor wanting to emerge. Even at an early age, I always loved the idea of being an actor, performer, or speaker.

My father nurtured this in me. As I said, he introduced me to the afternoon show, *Dark Shadows*. It was June of 1966 and I was eight years old. I came home from school one day and he said, *"I found a show that I think you are going to like. It's all about vampires and witches and scary things."* He was absolutely right. I was hooked from the moment Barnabas Collins entered through the doors of Collinwood until it ended it 1971. My father and I spent many afternoons watching *Dark Shadows*.

As I wonder why I loved scary movies, I can see it gave some normalcy to my home life. I was especially drawn to vampires and how they seemed to mirror some of my psychological drama at home. Just like the vampire who bit his victim and had complete control over him; likewise, I had psychological control over my father, biting him with compliments to appease him during his dark moments. In turn, his drinking and mental illness had control over all of us.

I was obsessed with *Dark Shadows*. It gave my brother more reason to dislike me since the walls on my side of the bedroom were plastered with *Dark Shadows* memorabilia. In contrast, I also had an altar with statues and candles where I prayed and tried to fulfill my promise to God in exchange for keeping my family safe from my father. As I spent my afternoons entertained by people coming out of graves and bloodthirsty vampires, at night I was lighting a candle at my altar for the starving kids in India, promising God I would become a priest if He kept Dad from killing Mom. I was so consumed with *Dark Shadows* that I never wanted to miss a show. In the summer months when we were out of school and playing baseball, I would ask someone the time so I could get to the TV in time to watch. I remember one instance where my friends lied to me about the time because we were in the middle of a game and they knew I would leave if they told me the truth. I was not happy when I found out I had missed an episode. In those days, there was no recording of shows or reruns of soap operas.

There was a specific time when my father truly became my hero. The actor who played Barnabas Collins (Jonathan Frid) was coming to the famous Winchester House in San Jose, California for an appearance. San Jose was about an hour and a half or so from our home. I begged my parents to take me to see him and get his autograph. Dad was my only ally on this venture and he convinced my mother to take me. *"It's important, Katie, for Frankie to meet the star of his favorite show."* I have a feeling he was just as excited as me to meet him.

The big day arrived for me to see Barnabas Collins. Would I be disappointed by my father pulling a drunk or some other crazy thing? It had become a pattern and a mental program for me to always think the other shoe was going to drop when I got excited about something good happening. Well, sure enough, something did happen and this time it was me and not my father. I woke up feeling sick on that special day. My mother said, *"You are not going anywhere this sick."*

"Please, please!" I begged, *"I have to see Barnabas. I will be better by the time we get there. I promise."*

My mother wouldn't relent and my father stepped in. *"Katie, he has his heart set on this day. You know how much he loves this show. Let's take him."*

This was quite the moment coming from a father who invented disappointing our family on a regular basis. My mother uneasily gave in with the stipulation that we would turn back if my condition worsened. I was so grateful to him in that moment for helping me live out my dream of meeting Barnabas Collins. On the way to San Jose, although I felt awful, I pretended not to be sick. I certainly didn't want us to turn around. I tried to sleep in the car. My usual red face was pale as a ghost.

We finally arrived at the event. It was hot and the line of parents and their kids went on forever. There must have been at least a thousand people there. I could see my mother's face was worn with worry but I was determined to stick it out. We got my ticket and got in that long line. I felt like we were in that line forever. I even got sick a couple more times, but I didn't care. My father saved my place while my mother took me to the bathroom. People were looking at us oddly. Were they feeling sorry for me or thinking I had bad parents for allowing me to stand in that line? As much as I usually cared what people thought, I surely didn't care this time. I was getting close to meeting the Vampire of Vampires. At one point, I felt really dizzy and sat down on a rock. I put my hands smack dab in the middle of a hornet's nest and was seriously stung. "*Enough!*" screamed my mother.

"*No, please, I am so close!*" I begged. "*Please, I am almost there.*"

Fortunately there was a nurse on site and she gave me something for the stings. I finally could see the door that would take me to Barnabas Collins. My father was actually behaving like a real father by caring for me and making this happen. Only two of us could enter so he told my mother to go get the car and he would take me the rest of the way. We would meet her in the parking lot.

I can remember walking into the dark room. There he

was, in the flesh, my favorite vampire. I could barely stand I was so weak. I handed my picture of him to autograph and he signed it. He didn't look enthused, but then I thought of how long he had to stand there greeting children. I wasn't disappointed. I saw his cool walking cane with the wolf on it and he was wearing his cool ring. He looked just like he did on TV. I had died and most definitely went to heaven, or maybe with a vampire, it was hell. Either way, I didn't care. I had lived my dream of meeting Barnabas Collins.

My father spoke, *"My son is a big fan. He went through a lot to see you today. He has been sick and he got stung by hornets to get to you. That's how much he likes you."*

Although I was embarrassed that my father told him I was sick and got stung, there was a part of me that felt good. My father was bragging on me and proud of me in a strange sort of way. Unmoved, Barnabas waved us on. I got my thirty seconds and I was as happy as a vampire in his coffin. I was not disappointed and the mission was accomplished. I thank my father for supporting my dream.

***

As I look back on the moments that my father was actually present, I am drawn to the memories of being a Cub Scout. I'm not sure how I landed in a Cub Scout troop. It wasn't like me. Perhaps it was recommended so that I would do more boy things. I remember that all the parents were required to take turns hosting a meeting in their homes. This caused incredible stress for me. My mother worked and she was not able to host. It would be left to my father when our turn came. Our home was a secret and I was never sure how my father was going to show up. Fortunately, my mother made some excuse as to why we were not able to host, and instead, provided refreshments for some of the meetings. The knots in my stomach disentangled with the assurance that our secret would not be exposed.

I do recall the famous Cub Scouts Pinewood Derby Races. It was a project designed for father and son bonding. I have to admit, this felt really awkward. My brother would have loved to do this with my father and I would have been happy to switch places with him. It felt fake because my father was absent in many ways. And now, were we going to be like all the other fathers and sons? How was this going to work out?

Dad never went to Danny's games or bonded with him. Why was this happening to me? How did I get roped into Cub Scouts to begin with? We couldn't tell the Scout leaders that my father wasn't really that kind of father. I convinced myself that maybe it would work out. After all, my father was a carpenter, and a good one, when he was present and sober. Once again, I can still feel the awkwardness of this father and son bonding.

We ordered the derby package and the date for the Pinewood Derby was chosen. We were committed. If you are not familiar with Pinewood Derbies, each car is built by a Cub Scout using a kit that includes a wooden block, plastic wheels, and metal axles. Trophies or medals are often awarded for the fastest car and the best designs. The package came in the mail and we had a month before the big race. If my memory serves me, my father found pictures in magazines of sport cars with possibilities for our design. My idea was to have a dragster like in the Indy 500 races. I did not watch races, but I had seen them on TV. It felt pretty cool and yet my trust issues were not there in regards to my father. In between his drinking binges and mental breakdowns, slowly but surely, the car started to take shape. Every day when I would come home from school, my father would have something new to show me. He had a great idea and I thought it was cool too. We had seen the race cars where the wheels are close together in front of the car and are further apart in the back. In the packet the wheels and axles were the same for the front and the back. My father said, *"No problem, I can extend the axle which will widen the tires in the back and make it look like a dragster car."*

"Wow! Dad is really trying," I thought to myself. I remember telling my mother how good Dad was doing. Oh, he was still getting drunk, but when we worked on the car he was all focused.

I remember varnishing the car as he coached me the whole way. We put stickers on it. It actually looked really cool. I was excited and we showed mother what we had done. My father felt good about it too. Did my excitement make him feel wanted? I might have been making that up, but in a sense, it made me feel good to know he felt good.

The Derby was scheduled on a Saturday morning. I felt confident that the chance of my father getting drunk and ruining the day for me was slim. Even if he got drunk the night before, he could be sober by morning. The big race arrived and I didn't care about winning or losing. I was just glad we made it to the day with no problems, embarrassments, or dramas. Mom came with us to witness the race. When we got there, the kids were already sharing their cars with each other. I was nervous. I was hesitant to introduce my father. It always felt awkward. We signed in and waited for our names to be called. The smell of competition was in the air. You could feel the anticipation from the racers and the family crowds watching. Our names were called and we were ready to begin.

The track was sloped and the cars ran only on the pull of

gravity. We each had our own track. We were instructed to place our car on the track. *"On your marks! Get set! Go!"* announced the person in charge. My car started down the slope. Then suddenly, it went off the track and hit other cars. Oh no! When my father had extended the axle on the back of the car, it did not fit the track. This was a big, big mistake. Everything was uniform in the package. We were instructed to design our cars as we wished, but we had to use the exact material we were given. We had not followed the directions and our car did not fit on the track. I was disqualified and they stopped the race and started again without me. I was mortified and embarrassed. People were trying to be nice to us. *"Your Derby car still looked really cool!"* I walked away to stand by my parents. I wanted to leave but we waited for the winners to be announced and the ceremony to be over. Of course I was mad at my father for embarrassing me. He should have known better. Once again, I repeated the pattern of being disappointed. I did not know at the time but I was always setting myself up for disappointment.

Now, as an adult, I realize it wasn't my father's fault. We just didn't follow the directions. It happens to all of us. Unfortunately, at eight, I had to blame someone. My father gave me plenty reasons to blame him, but in this case, he did the best he could. He meant for me to have the greatest car. The Pinewood Derby holds a good memory for me, even with the mortifying ending. My father really showed up for me and supported me and my short stay with the Cub Scouts. Maybe that was the only reason for being a Cub Scout because I had no intention of moving forward with the Boy's Scouts of America.

***

As I continue my journey down memory lane in search of the "Good Father," I am reminded that it is all perception. I am grateful to find a good moment or two within the darkness of my father's severe struggle with mental illness.

I am not sure when I decided I wanted to be an actor or performer, but I remember my father supported that dream. When I entered St. David's School as the new kid in second grade, I was very shy. I would be asked to read out loud and I would hide behind my book, speaking so softly that I could not be heard. Sister Joan Therese would yank the book out of my hands and throw it across the floor. *"Pick up that book, Frankie, and come to the front of the class and read out loud. Don't hide behind that book! Let me see your face when you read!"*

"Yes, Sister Joan Therese," I said with a high-pitched voice and a very red face. I was so embarrassed. The kids were all snickering but I'm sure they were probably scared for me and themselves at the same time. I picked up that book and I looked out at that sea of faces. I began to read. That was the day I found my voice. I do not believe I ever shut up again after that. Later, when I would get scolded and scolded for speaking in class, I am sure that nun regretted that day she freed my voice.

It was at this young age, I started to think about wanting to be an actor. I thought about how performing might be fun. It would be a way to be seen. I think I liked being seen. After all, at home I lived in the shadow of my older brother. I also discovered that people like to laugh. As time went on, I discovered I had a natural gift in making people laugh, much to the dismay of my teachers. By the time I was in the third grade, I was most definitely coming out of my shyness. So much so that my third-grade teacher, Mrs. Bush, gave my name to the principal to be Master of Ceremonies for our yearly talent show. It was a big deal at school. Everyone attended — parents, teachers, and students. I was surprised that I would be considered. It was unheard of that a third-grader would host an evening so important. Normally, only an eighth-grader would be selected.

The Principal, Sister Margaret Marie, had many meetings with Mrs. Bush and me. I don't recall how it happened but I was picked to be Master of Ceremonies. I was nervous and my stomach turned beforehand, but once I got out there in front of an audience, I was never so alive. I did well and everyone was happy about the choice except for those who thought I was favored. There was much competition in school, but mostly between parents wanting their children to be noticed. I was most definitely bit by the performing bug.

Here is another fond memory in search of a "Good Father." Ever since Sister Joan Therese yanked that book out of my hands, I continued to be pulled toward acting, speaking, directing, and producing. At eight years old, another opportunity for me to follow that growing dream came through a commercial I saw on TV. The spokesperson was Paul Peterson from *The Donna Reed Show*. He was telling us to call in and come down to be a star. Auditions were being held in San Francisco. I wrote down the number. He said they were looking for exceptional young people. Of course I knew that was me. After all, I played the flying monkey in *The Wizard of Oz*, which I directed and produced in third grade. Naturally, I was ready to take flight as an actor and performer. I asked my mother if I could go to the audition. I knew she couldn't get off work but I had to try. She told me it was just a way to get our money. "*It's a scam,*" she said. I didn't believe her. After all, it was Donna Reed's son and I knew it had to be real. This commercial had to be trusted. How young at heart and trusting an eight-year-old can be. What I remember about me as a child is when I got excited about something I wanted, I was unstoppable. I had determination. If I could navigate my father through his craziness, I had to be able to get an audition in San Francisco.

My father was aware of how much it meant to me and he offered to be my ally and take me to the audition. My mother insisted it was a trick. Compounding this was her fear of me riding in the car with my father because of the probability of his drinking. I kept assuring her it was real and my father would be okay. The answer was final, "*No!*" she said. "*End of story!*" I was so disappointed, but my father took notice of this and talked to me privately. "*I'm going to take you,*" he said, "*but we are not gonna tell Mom.*"

As a child, I cannot remember going against my mother. She was my sole authority. However, this time, I justified going with my father because I was convinced if I went there, I could prove to my mother that it was for real. I would become a child star. I believed it with my whole heart. You see, I believed in my acting career so much that I wrote Dan Curtis, the Producer of *Dark Shadows*, and let him know that if the little boy who currently played David wasn't able to do the part, I would like to audition for the role.

I was always visualizing new adventures. Although the fear of disappointment caused by my father's drinking and mental episodes lingered in the back of my mind, I still would go forward with joyous excitement for the possibility of a happy ending. Disappointment or not, I had to take this chance. I had my father call the number I had written down from the TV commercial and he made the appointment for me. I admit it was hard to lie to my mother, but this eight-year-old knew it was for the greater good. My acting career could change everything.

At last, audition day was here. I scrutinized my father's behavior to make sure he was the good father that morning and that he wasn't sneaking booze before we left. He had hiding places for his booze all over the house. I was like a detective always finding them in the strangest places. Interestingly, I wasn't as afraid of him driving drunk as I was of him embarrassing me in front of the movie people. It was summer so I was out of school. Off we went, over the Bay Bridge and into the city for my big break. We found a parking space easily. My stomach started to get a million butterflies. I wanted to be there but suddenly my fear and shyness reemerged. My father gave me advice. *"Be just as you are at home — funny and entertaining. You have nothing to be afraid of."*

I was still nervous but we got out of the car and went inside. There were lots of kids and it was very exciting. There were movie posters that lined the walls. It was just as I imagined — very Hollywood. I was checked in and my picture was taken with a polaroid camera. They gave my father a form to fill out. I knew he had trouble filling out forms so I took it from him and completed it the best I could. My name was called and in we went to the meeting. They asked me about my experience. Very proudly, I told them I had played the flying monkey in the Wizard of Oz and that I had directed the play too. They let me know that I had a good look but I needed camera experience and acting classes. This was the perfect place for me to do that. I could feel the energy shift. *"How much are these classes going to cost?"* Dad asked. I don't remember the amount but I knew it was more than we could ever afford. *"We'll think about it,"* said Dad. *"I need to discuss it with his mom."*

The movie folks assured us there were very few spots left and that we should make up our minds soon. I think they asked for a deposit. My father refused. I was not embarrassed but extremely disappointed. I am not sure if I was more dejected because it was not what I had created in my mind, or because my mother was right about it being a scam. On the way home, my father told me there would be other chances and they wouldn't cost me money. He let me know it was not the end. I think he took me to McDonald's Hamburgers to make me feel better. Food always seemed to be the great comforter when things would go wrong. A milkshake, burger, and some fries lessened the sting of my first disappointment in show business.

I did end up telling my mother that I went to San Francisco and that Dad took me. I asked her not to be mad at Dad. I told her it was all my fault because I begged him to do it. *"Please don't tell him I told you, Mom."* I didn't want him to know I told on him. To be honest, I think it gave my father and me a strange moment of bonding. I apologized to my mother and admitted that she was right about the scam. She was fine with it and was glad that I told her. My father came through for me but I knew it was only a matter of time that the other father would come out to torture the family. It is nice to have some memories of my father that were good.

***

Speaking of food, another good memory of my father was having secret barbeques with him during the day. Our family had had a financial windfall with my father's settlement from the accident at his job at Jacuzzi Pumps. With the extra finances, my parents bought a freezer and thought it would be economically sound to buy half a cow to have in the freezer. Supposedly, you saved money by having all that meat cut up and ready to go. On some days after school, my father would say, "*Do you want a steak or a burger? We can barbeque them.*" I was all in for that. "*Yes!*" I'd shout, and into the freezer he went to get our meat. Some kids get milk and cookies after school. I got an early dinner.

Sometimes we would have this barbeque late in the afternoon and we could not tell Mom for two reasons. Firstly, she would be upset we weren't hungry for the dinner she'd cooked. Secondly, she would not be pleased that we were eating meat so casually. It was expensive and we were always on a budget. As usual, my mother found out and let my father know how unhappy she was with us eating like kings when she was at work. Nevertheless, I still have good memories of those secret barbeques with my father.

***

When I was around twelve years old, a San Francisco theatrical opportunity presented itself. My father stepped in to make sure I got there to this interview/audition. This time my mother was on board because it was with a legitimate agent. There were no gimmicks; just a meeting to see if they might want to represent me. I got this interview because I'd looked up theatrical agents in the phone book. There were three in the city. I wrote them each a letter and sent in a picture of myself. One of those three agencies called me in.

I was so excited and scared at the same time. Would I get an agent? When I met the head agent, he said the reason he called me in was because of the honesty in my letter. He said he'd never before had anyone so proud of playing the flying monkey in *The Wizard of Oz*. My passion for acting was so obvious, he just had to give me a meeting. He gave me a commercial to read. Then, he took some time to explain how tough showbiz was. "*There's more noes than yeses,*" he emphasized. *"If you can do anything else other than pursue acting, I suggest you do it."* His advice seemed to come from a caring place. I told him I loved it and I felt like it was something I was good at it. I realized I didn't have a lot of experience but it didn't matter to me.

My father said very little. Then the agent asked him how he liked the idea of his son wanting to pursue acting. He answered something like this, *"Acting is all he thinks about and he is quite an entertainer at home. He was so excited when he got your letter, he's thought of nothing else."*

As someone who has spent much of his life pursuing and working in theater and film, I know it is not easy for someone to really take notice of you. This audition was a big deal and my father was genuinely happy for me. I always wondered what was the real underlying glue that created what I considered to be a bond between my father and me. Was my ability to calm him at those times of his intoxication and anger the basis of this relationship? Perhaps it was. I do believe he could trust me. Although I longed to, I could not trust him on any level. On the other hand, I believe it is very healthy for one to try and point out the good, if and when we can find it, and that is what I have tried to do within these pages. I am sure I have made it quite clear by now that I had two different fathers in one body.

***

When my father got his settlement for his injury at Jacuzzi pumps, he gave my mother and I each $100 to go shopping at El Cerrito Plaza. That was a lot back in 1968. I remember him dropping us both off at the shopping center. I could tell he genuinely loved watching us go off that night with $100 bills in each of our hands. Where did my father go? I would imagine to a nearby bar to do what he loved to do. I didn't care. I had $100 to spend on myself. My mother gave me a time and place to meet and we went off in different directions. When I made my first purchase and broke the hundred-dollar bill and got the change back, I felt even richer. I loved the feeling of being able to buy anything I wanted. I had my little wallet and I was a big spender. I was beside myself. I remember buying bell bottom pants, shirts, Calvin Klein jeans, a Nancy Sinatra Album, and much more, including candy of course.

I'll always remember that evening provided by my father. When you come from a family that is always watching what they spend, it is a treat to have no restrictions like I did that night. I came home with a little money left over and hands filled with packages. I felt like one of the rich kids from the East Richmond Heights.

My father used to say to my mother, "*You love money, Katie. Your eyes light up when you have money.*"

"*That's because I see so little of it,*" she'd respond.

***

I was terrified of math. I just froze at numbers when a problem was presented to me to solve. I could not get my brain to understand it. What was wrong with me? My father, with a fourth- grade education, did not contribute a lot to my world of academia, but as a carpenter he had some math skills from which I benefitted. Then something happened to math in the 1960s. It was called "New Math."

> *This dreaded and traumatic change in the teaching of basic mathematics had young kids pondering abstract algebra, modular*

arithmetic, matrices, symbolic logic, Boolean algebra, and other super-math stuff they might never need."

- GROOVYHISTORY.COM; 2018

It was quite the big deal to me when the letter came home requesting one or both of my parents to attend New Math classes with me so they could assist me with my homework. These requests always made me feel uncomfortable, and for good reason. My family would be invaded and our secret would be found out. My mother was willing to go but she admitted she wasn't good at math and was not sure she could really help me. My father offered to go. *"Looking at this New Math might be interesting."* Then, he added, *"What's wrong with the old Math?"*

So, both parents were on board. My usual and only concern was how do I keep my father from drinking before we go? After all, it was night and that was usually when our household went south with his alcoholism. For weeks I would worry about this upcoming night. Would my father act up in front of all the other parents and the teachers? There was enough proof available that made this probable. New Math night finally arrived and my father seemed fine. There were coffee and refreshments for us at the event. Some of the other parents came up to introduce themselves. *"We're so happy to meet you finally,"* they said to my father. *"We've missed you at church on Sundays."* This was definitely a putdown and I was embarrassed. Neither my father or mother commented on the remark.

I felt that both my parents really tried hard to understand the introduction to New Math so they could help me. I, on the other hand, was just confused, freezing up with every math problem presented. My mother understood a little but did not feel she could be a lot of help. To my surprise, the good father did understand a lot of it. He even asked and answered questions from the nun that was teaching the class. I found myself experiencing a new emotion for him. I was proud of him.

Well, the first night went well. The school called for two more sessions. Of course that meant more anxiety for me. For some reason my mother wasn't worried and sent my father with me to finish out those classes. I did feel good and there was a moment in the church hall with all those parents, kids, and teachers that I felt normal, instead of an outsider in my community.

***

Although the bad times seem to outweigh the good, I have highlighted some of the good memories of my father. I always felt I was pushing the cart uphill when it came to him and the uncertainty surrounding our relationship. I always tried to look at the positive. I do know he was doing the best he could with the cards that were dealt.

How does it come about that a little child decides to look at the brighter side of life? Was it modeled somewhere in my upbringing? I know my mother seemed to enjoy life in the midst of all the drama. When my father was sober and sane, he seemed to look at life somewhat positively. There is always good to be found when we go looking for it. I discovered some good memories, and though they may be few, they can buffer some of the pain a young boy endured when living with mental illness and alcoholism.

My Window of Opportunity

"If a window of opportunity appears, don't pull down the shade."

- TOM PETERS

"Why don't you just move to Los Angeles now?" My mother's voice was calm and direct.

"What?" I could not believe my ears.

"You can finish your schooling there just as easily as here and you can get a job there just as easily as well," she continued.

"What about you Mom? I can't leave you by yourself. Dad could act up at any time."

"It is only a six-hour drive and a one-hour flight. I will be fine and I certainly can handle Dad," she said with a confident tone.

"Are you sure Mom?"

"Yes, I am sure. I think it is the best thing for you. I will feel better knowing you are not in this rough town."

My mother was literally greenlighting (a Hollywood term) my dream of becoming an actor. One factor that helped awaken me to that dream was when I was around twelve years old. My mother, father, and I went to Los

Angeles on vacation. We went to Disneyland and Universal Studios. I recall my father was on his best behavior. Before we headed back to San Pablo, we stayed the night at a Travel Lodge on Sunset Boulevard. While my parents slept, I was awake. I couldn't stop looking out the window of our hotel room. My heart was racing with excitement at the billboards and marquees of current movies that lined the Boulevard. I remember sitting at that little desk in the room, writing in my journal, "*Someday I will be back and I will live in Hollywood and become an actor.*"

I was nineteen when my mother gave me that okay. I had an agent and had booked a few commercials, but San Pablo was not Hollywood. I often wondered if I'd be destined to live there forever. After all, I had a huge list of reasons why I shouldn't go. Firstly, and most importantly, there was my home drama. My mother had finally separated from my father. He wasn't living in the house, but he frequently visited our home on Sundays. My childhood nightmare of my father and what he was capable of still lingered over us like a bad dream. There was also the threat of my brother Danny who was diagnosed bipolar and could become quite violent. Then there was college. I was attending Contra Costa Junior College in San Pablo. I was taking psychology classes and I loved them. By taking this leap of faith, I would give up the dependable career I was pursuing in Criminal Justice as a probation officer. I had justified giving up my dream for stability. I'd always told myself I liked working with kids. This would be an okay career. Also, all my eighteen and nineteen-year-old friends were getting married. Hollywood might be calling but I was engaged to a girl I'd met at college. How was I going to tell my fiancé I want to move to Los Angeles?

My head was spinning. My dream was quite persistent and my mother had said to go, but I was engaged, as well as working —selling shoes, cleaning houses, doing theater, going to college. Would I settle in my hometown and never go after my dream? These were all the questions I was asking of myself. Deep within, I knew I had to go. I would never be satisfied until I made this leap of faith. I finally had the courage to tell my fiancé.

She was shocked. "*I don't want to move to Los Angeles.*" Her answer had a finality about it but I continued to tell her all the good things that could happen there.

"*It will be an adventure,*" I said.

My fiancé had a sister that had moved back home from Hollywood. I loved talking to her and hearing about all the experiences she had in Tinsel Town. She was on my side. However, my fiancé wouldn't budge. I continued to contemplate what it would mean to stay in San Pablo. I wouldn't realize my lifelong dream and I would continue to be stuck in my home drama. I just *had* to take advantage of this opportunity.

I approached my fiancé for what I knew would be the last time. "*I am going to move with or without you. I have to take this opportunity.*" I meant it and she knew it. She agreed to go.

I don't think she really wanted to go. I think she wanted to be with me. Her sister decided she would join us. I reminded them all that there was nothing holding us here in San Pablo and a whole new world was waiting for us. We waited a bit, finishing out the school year and saving as much money as we could. Finally, we gave notice at our jobs. It was time to go. I left with only my clothes and a Hollywood Dream. I liken the three of us to that sitcom, *Three's Company*, with John Ritter, Suzanne Sommers, and Joyce Dewitt. We were perfectly cast.

I remember saying goodbye to my mother. I promised her I'd call and I could be home anytime she needed me. There wasn't a lot of emotion on her part. She was quiet. At one point, later on I called home because things weren't working out as well as I thought. Her voice on the other side of the line said, "*Just stay another week. Things will work out.*" Later on, my father told me she cried when we hung up the phone on that day.

I do not regret taking that window of opportunity and I thank my mother for encouraging me not to quit. The Little Man would become the prince of his dreams and nothing was going to stop him. I remember going over what we called the Grapevine on Highway 5 with my heart beating. I screamed out, "*Hollywood here we come, ACTION!*" But the first stop was San Fernando Valley! *CUT!* (There is a whole new story starting here and must be saved for another book or movie.)

SPOILER ALERT! The boy and girl and sister from San Pablo did start a Hollywood life filled with adventure; some good, and some not so good. Patrick and the girl were engaged for five years and never did say, "*I do!*" The good news is she ended up loving Los Angeles, doing very well, and marrying the man that was truly right for her. So right, she is still with him today. Her sister is doing fine as well.

Behind the Mask
Hypersensitivity
and Other Magical
Powers

"Wearing a mask wears you out. Faking it is fatiguing. The most exhausting activity is pretending to be what you know you aren't."

– RICK WARREN

It would be many years and into adulthood before I discovered and understood the superhero powers that carried me through my childhood. I would begin to unpack that discovery in my quest to be a working actor in Los Angeles. Every part of our life reveals a gift, if we are open to receiving it. Mine came in putting on the costume of Spiderman. I landed the very cool gig of touring the world as Spiderman for Marvel Comics. My appearances as the webslinger included ten years of parade appearances, signing comic books, receiving the keys to various cities, pitching the first ball at National Baseball games and even making appearances with Stan Lee himself. Throwing the opening pitch was quite a surprise turn of events for the boy who lived in the shadow of his star athlete brother.

I auditioned for the role in New York City. The casting director had called me in to play Captain America. However, she noted right away that Captain America, standing stoically with shield in hand, was a waste of my energetic personality. *"You might make a better Spiderman,"* she said as she handed me a one piece, zip-across-the-back nylon Spidey suit. Excited at this possibility of portraying one of my childhood heroes, off I went to change! As I slipped the suit over the lower part of my body, I could see that nothing would be left to the imagination. I was not heavy at age thirty, but still, I had to suck in my stomach to make sure I presented perfectly to the producers. As I slipped the last of that tight-fitting material over my head, I was surprised I could even breathe. It was the tiny netted hole over my nose and mouth that made it possible. I took a deep breath and looked at myself in the mirror. Yes, I felt quite at home in this personality I was destined to wear until I was forty years old. Wow! I never thought of myself as a physical superhero.

I didn't waste any time. I wanted this role. As soon as they called me into the audition room, I fearlessly jumped on to the producer's desk, shooting out imaginary webs. After only moments, there was no doubt in anyone's mind. I would fly around the world as Spiderman. For ten years I did just that, but it wasn't until a very special project came up that I would truly learn how the Universe shows up to assist us in our healing. A comic book was created to support Child Abuse Prevention.

> *"In 1984, the National Committee for the Prevention of Child Abuse, with Marvel Comics, created a one-shot Spiderman/Power Pack comic in which it is revealed that Peter Parker was molested by Steven "Skip" Westcott, a teenage boy from a broken home."*
>
> *-VCU LIBRARIES, SOCIAL HISTORY WELFARE HISTORY PROJECT HTTPS://IMAGES.SOCIALWELFARE.LIBRARY.VCU. EDU/ITEMS/SHOW/368*

That comic book went on tour with me as Spidey. Into the public school system we went, along with social workers who stood by to take care of the children. As Spidey, I would disclose being sexually abused by my older friend when I was Peter Parker. I not only spoke on sexual abuse, but verbal and physical abuse as well. Those auditoriums were packed with hundreds, sometimes thousands of kids. As Spidey told his story, you could hear a pin drop.

The brilliance of Marvel Comics bringing a superhero down to the level of the experiences of some of those kids never failed. The message Spidey gave at event after event was to let someone know if you were being hurt or doing something that didn't feel good.

"*You are not alone,*" said Spidey in earnest. "*There are loving people to help you.*"

Many children revealed their own abuse, opening the door for the social workers to step in and further investigate their individual stories. Hidden behind the mask, it was my gift to tell the story that I knew firsthand. At the same time, I was helping thousands of kids reveal their possible abuse because Spiderman was an example of what one could become regardless of circumstances. If he could do it, they could too. I felt honored to assist in this way. I remember one little boy coming up to me and whispering, "*I'm sorry about what happened to you Spiderman, but you turned out all right.*"

The social workers at the events recognized my strength in telling the story and would call in extra social workers at my events because many more kids would disclose. At one event I had an exchange with one of the social workers. She expressed her gratitude for me and for the program. "*A lot of children are helped and saved from continued abuse because your heart shines through with true authenticity and authority,"* she said. Then she added, *"It must be comforting for you to be able to disclose behind the mask of a superhero and feel safe."*

I pretended to be unclear about what she was saying. Instead, I smiled, merely said thank you and excused myself. I was on the clock and it was a bit insensitive on her part to try to draw me out like that. As I sat with her comment later, I wondered, *"Was she leaving the conversation open for me to disclose? If I hadn't been working, would I have revealed my secret?"* I realized in that moment it was more about how I felt when she made the comment. Was there still a part of me hiding and protecting my family in my thirties? I don't think I even knew the answer to that question then.

I am very clear on how the Universal Power that brings our experiences to us based on our thoughts and feelings will always find a way to conspire in our favor. Yes, that day, beyond that social worker's comment, I began to realize my magical powers that carried me through my childhood. I lived behind the mask too. As a kid, I lived two lives; my public life and my home life. I had superpowers that kept my out-in-the-world personality intact, light, carefree, and humorous, while another part of me was at home living with and dealing with my father's emotional abuse and many personalities. I was able to keep his personalities straight in my own little mind. In order to keep myself and my family safe, I knew how to communicate with each one. I always recognized the sane father, the sober father, the one I loved in spite of it all. You see, when my father was not drunk and angry, he was a nice guy, a normal guy. However, when the other personalities came out, I was always ready. Just like Spiderman, I had the superpower of hypersensitivity. It allowed me to make important decisions at just the right time. I could read and feel my father in order to be ready in any moment to protect myself and my mother and brother. I do not believe hypersensitivity — also known as being a *"highly sensitive person"* (HSP) — is a disorder like some claim. I believe it is a gift.

> *"Symptoms of hypersensitivity include being highly sensitive to the physical (via sound, sight, touch, or smell and/or emotional stimuli and the tendency to be easily overwhelmed by too much information."* - Merriam Webster Dictionary

How is hypersensitivity a superpower? A hypersensitive person picks up on more information within and around themselves and processes that information more deeply, which means their intuition is highly developed. I had this hypersensitivity for as long as I can consciously remember. I do wonder if I was born with it or if it was birthed out of fear; a survival mechanism. What I do know is that this foundation allowed me to rise above my circumstances and environment. I had the ability to pick up on every sense: sight, hearing, smell, taste, and touch in magnified ways.

> *"You know how Superman can hear the tiniest pin drop from far away? It's almost like having superhero senses without the superspeed or the ability to fly"* - Brittney Blount

Yep, that was me; the Little Man who knew how to use his intuitive power to be one step ahead of the man who might do anything in any moment, including kill me or hurt me severely. My vigilant alertness, that adrenalin shooting off continually, makes me wonder how I had an unshattered nerve left in my body. I was so sensitive to my father, I felt like

I was a part of him. Every facial move he made was a signal of what he might do next. My ability to feel him stirring emotionally as he sat in his chair saved me from physical harm on many occasions. I knew immediately when another energy would come through. I remember thinking, *"Dad's gone again."*

No one else in the house was tuned into Dad like this, but for me it was a matter of life and death to read my father. When I felt it, it caused goose bumps on my arms and the hair on the back of my neck would stand on end. I could have easily become paralyzed but I would force myself not to freeze, but to be ready to run. As I write these words, my body is experiencing the same tingling sensation of fear that I felt on those occasions over fifty years ago. As I later studied the work of Dr. Joe Dispenza, I would learn that those emotions are still stored in the body. I would learn that it was important for me to face them, address them, and release them in order to go on and create a new life, freed from the past. Unconscious about this for a long time, I recreated those disempowering moments through dysfunctional relationships.

Was little Patrick a superhero? I think he was. He did his best to protect his family and himself. His nervous system was tested full throttle as a child growing up in a war zone. I continue to wonder how big a price I paid to earn these superpowers cultivated for survival. I know that I am extremely grateful for my hypersensitivity. However, I needed to learn through therapy and spiritual practice to calm my hypersensitivity down, as it did not serve me as I grew into a man who wanted to be in healthy relationship with others both on an intimate level and in the workplace.

See No Evil: The Long Road to Diagnosis

"It seems to me it's always the evil we refuse to see that does us the greatest harm."

-ROBERT B. BAER

The subject of my father's mental diagnosis and care is what I will attempt to address here. It might well be a question that many readers have on their minds. However, if you know anything about mental illness in our country, you will know that accessing care is difficult for many reasons.

> *"The behavioral health crisis in the United States has never been more apparent. The COVID-19 public health emergency laid bare the intensity of need for behavioral health services. In a recent survey, 23.8% of Americans with symptoms of anxiety or a depressive disorder had unmet mental health needs. That's an increase of 2.8% from August 2020." -bcbsnc.com*

My father was in and out of the mental wards of Veterans' Hospitals throughout my life. The timetable of his admittances and returns to our home are a bit confusing. I will do my best to piece it together in a coherent way for you, the reader.

When I was a small child, my father would have severe

mental episodes that would cause him to be admitted to those mental wards. Those episodes would last a certain amount of time, and then he would appear to be normal again and he would be released. The revolving door went on for most of my life until he was finally admitted for a permanent stay at Palo Alto Veterans Hospital. This final diagnosis came when he was considered to be a threat to himself and society. Didn't they know he was always a threat to himself and his family? Of course not, because we added to the dilemma by using our energy to cover up what went on at home.

Without a definite diagnosis, the mental wards became more of a place for my father to dry out from alcohol. Although the doctors might mention that he had PTSD, in the end it was always attributed to his drinking. My mother did take him to the Veterans Hospital for a checkup when he got "really bad," but they would only keep him until he "became himself again." I enjoyed those respites from his rages, but they were short-lived.

As I remember, he would make a few visits to the mental wards when I was really young, but as I got to be eight or nine, he became much worse and it was apparent he was beyond the bottle. When he would go on a week or two-week long rage, it was obvious we could not handle him. We were in fear of being killed, so he would finally be arrested and jailed or taken back to the Veterans Hospital for psychiatric care or drying out.

During the Vietnam Era, my mother got so fed up with him not holding a job, she insisted he go into the Merchant Marines. They actually accepted him despite the fact they knew about his mental episodes. I must have been around nine years old and I remember us taking him to the docks where he was shipping out. Mom, Danny, and I stood there waving as the ship left. I felt such joy in my heart. I would be free from my father for at least a while. As I looked over at my brother, I saw how sad he was, as if he were losing his best friend. We were two brothers in the same household with opposite feelings. As for my mother, she looked relieved to have him leave. We were free and safe. I remember the peace that was in our home when he was gone. I could be a normal kid. I felt as though all my time on my knees begging for help was finally answered. My dream was shattered when a couple of months after he left, my mother got a call that my father had experienced a breakdown. A bombing where he was stationed triggered a psychotic episode. He was in the mental ward and would be returned home as soon as he was stable. When my mother told us he would be returning, I felt a wave of emotionally overwhelming disappointment.

"I'm so sad and angry, Mom. I don't want him to come home!" I cried.

"Let's just enjoy the time we have until he gets back." That was all she could give me in the way of comfort. It was her standard answer in our times of my father's absence.

What kind of life was that? My father might be in a prison of his mind, but was I destined to be a prisoner for my whole childhood? There were so many times when my young heart doubted we'd ever make it through my father's returns. When he returned from Vietnam, he was definitely severely shell-shocked. Whatever happened to him there made him even worse. He continued drinking and his different personalities were completely exposed, and yet it was still disguised as a rage due to alcohol. He seemed to be needing more alcohol and stronger doses. He went from red port wine to whiskey. The alcohol might have helped keep the demons at bay, but his temper seemed to become more intense. My Spidey senses made me hyper-attuned to know the worst was yet to come.

I remember playing the popular song, *Those Were the Days* by Mary Hopkin, on my record player. That one song made him ballistic. "*Turn it off, turn it off. Goddamn it, turn that fucking thing off now,*" as he broke my record in half.

"*Get on the floor! Duck! Duck! Those sons of bitches know I am here and they are afraid I will tell everything!*" He was obviously terrified.

As his paranoia got worse, my mother continued to take him to the Veterans Hospital where he was admitted for short stays until he would be himself again. The doctors would say, "*He is back but I am not sure for how long.*"

My curiosity as a child wondered what the doctor meant by, "*He's back.*" I always wondered where he had gone and what he did or thought when in that state. I never asked. I didn't think they'd tell a young boy. Instead, I just endured and prayed for our safety. My father was getting worse, and still the Veterans Administration would not fully diagnose and commit him. Perhaps since my mother and the family were still guarding and protecting him, there was no reason for them to step in. The army therapists he saw began to prescribe drugs they said would calm his nerves. They were called nerve pills in those days. I'm not sure they helped him at all.

As for the Little Man, I still knew how to calm him down in the darkness of the bedroom, with the smell of stale alcohol and Pall Mall cigarettes glowing in the dark. I wondered how he did not burn the place down as those cigarettes lingered haphazardly on the edge of those ashtrays, about to fall off. They would edge their way to the corner of the ashtray, ready to drop. I seemed to arrive just in time to catch that cigarette. These times, though more intense, were no different than those of earlier episodes. They always began with him calling out for my mother. At the sound of "*Katie!*" my mission to get him to fall asleep began. As time went on, he seemed to get a little rougher with me. He would hold me so tight against his body I was not sure I could escape. However, I knew if I were to get trapped, I could call out to my mother. I tried not to go to that bedroom if my mother was not home, but if I had to, I made sure I had an escape plan in place. It was a lot of strategic planning for such a young child.

My puberty years seem to be the hardest for me. My body was going through changes. I was sweating and had a different smell than before. It seemed more difficult to be the appeaser. My mother reminded me not to speak of what I was going through during puberty because my father would make fun of me. I wasn't always good at hiding it. She was right. He taunted me vulgarly, "*Do you have hair on your balls yet? Let me see if you're a man yet?*"

I hated his taunts more than ever, and because I was getting bigger, I felt tempted to defend myself on the physical level. I never did. I was too afraid of making even more trouble for my family. One night my father got so out of control that I had to call the police again. When they arrived, he became the perfectly calm husband and father. On some level he knew how to manipulate his surroundings and the people in them. That was when something changed in me in regards to what I knew about him. Did he have personalities that stood alone and could they actually take over his body and mind?

As I was finishing my seventh and eighth grade education at St. David's, the continuous nights of my father's rage finally brought my mother to a breaking point. She was actually seriously considering divorce. She went to get the help of a lawyer. The lawyer asked her if she planned to remarry. "*Oh God, no!*" she replied. The lawyer advised her to get a legal separation because then she wouldn't lose the benefit of his pension. In the world of form, it was the best advice she could have received. Her long sentence of living with this man would eventually give her security in her later years. The separation would ultimately lead to the paperwork that would get my father the help he needed.

My father's stays at the mental hospital were longer now. He was monitored and medicated, but still not fully diagnosed. He was free to come and go and would visit my mother on the weekends. She would take him for rides in the car and they would have ice cream outings together. At times his behavior was like a little boy with his mother. I was already out of the house when my mother set him up in his own place in Oakland. After the separation, she became his conservator; a job she had done for him for their whole marriage.

As I had my whole life, I helped him in other ways. My mother thought it might help if I spoke to him. "*He will listen to you,*" she pleaded. I didn't want to go, but I'd go for her. I visited him in his new home in a very scary part of Oakland. It became more about counseling for me. You see, he craved a false sense of independence for once in his life and he felt my mother was blocking that for him. She was buying his groceries and checking on him on her lunch breaks. She took care of all his needs while he just sat in his place staring into space or watching TV. I made it clear that Mom only treated him like a child because that was the way he was acting.

Well, he would soon lose all his independence forever. He was still getting drunk, and the finale to this chapter came when he started a fire in his home. Finally, after all the years of torture of trying to find an answer and help with his mental illness, I believe the Veterans Administration realized he was a danger to himself and society. It was apparent that my father could not be on his own and it was time to admit him on a more permanent basis.

The doctors finally did diagnose him with paranoid schizophrenia, delusions, personality disorder, and other mental illnesses. Paranoid schizophrenia was the winning diagnosis (yes, I say that with sarcasm) that would finally get him admitted to a mental hospital permanently. They put him on some strong medication to assist with the schizophrenia. Haloperidol (Haldol) and Perphenazine (Trilafon) were the ones I remembered. The challenge was that the medications would keep him calm for a certain time period and then he would become immune to them. The personality disorder and violent raging would return. This cycle of changing his medication went on for years. The doctors and psychiatrists let us know that if my father went out too far mentally that he may never fully return to any kind of normalcy of the man we knew. This was not shocking to me. I had not seen my real father for a very long time.

My father was admitted in the mid-1980s for a permanent residency. We were advised that I should become his conservator and manage his financial affairs instead of my mother. We agreed. Although I was living in New York City and Los Angeles pursuing an acting career, I could handle it because there wasn't much for me to manage. The Veterans Hospital in Menlo Park took care of most of his basic needs. He was responsible for additional items such as cigarettes, spending money, underwear, and personal toiletries. He was diagnosed as one-hundred percent disabled and was financially compensated. He now had the money he needed to live as he wished. How ironic that he now made a decent living but was not living a full life to spend it. I would visit him when I was home or when necessary for a hospital meeting. My mother visited him almost every Sunday.

In the beginning of his now permanent stay, he would escape occasionally and find his way to our mobile home park. That was a bit scary for my mother. I remember her driving him back herself after he had escaped. My mother had a lot of faith to subject herself to a man who was capable of anything in any moment.

I wasn't sure if I was going to add this part to the book, and yet intuitively, I feel it is an important part of my father's journey and mine. If I am going to be as truthful as possible, I must be transparent. When I would visit my father, they would unlock the doors and he would usually be brought to us, or we would meet him in the main section where all the patients could be visible and monitored by the nurses. My father's state of mind and behavior would be either somewhat catatonic, or he could be talkative and appear as normal. Even though it might take a moment or two, he would recognize me most of the time. When I would first see him, I would give him a hug and a kiss on the cheek. There were many times when this clearly agitated him and he would become almost frightened like a child.

"Men don't do that," he would repeat over and over to me.

"Fine, Dad, I won't do that again." I proceeded to calm him, as I was trained to do. How ironic that he yelled at me for kissing him when I spent a childhood being forced to appease and kiss him. I wondered many times as I witnessed this behavior that perhaps my father was gay. Maybe this explained that sexual feeling I felt when I was in bed with him as a young boy. My father never penetrated me or touched me sexually with his hands, but there was a definite feeling of sexual contact when he pressed his body against me and rubbed my face with his. How did he resist the urge to go further?

I received the answer, when later in life, I found out from my mother that he was impotent early in their marriage. This explained why they were never fully intimate. My mother revealed that she spent a lot of time wondering what was wrong with her, because after a few years of marriage, he would never touch her. It truly affected her personality and she never really felt attractive. My father's insults didn't help her either.

My Spidey senses definitely told me there was a sexual demon haunting him along with all the other demons from his abusive childhood and the devastating results of his time in the war. Does this matter? — only to a Little Man that wanted to understand the abusive jungle of his childhood. I would often think if this sexual confusion was one of my father's demons and he was gay, how sad it was that he never came to embrace his sexuality. That might have saved him in the end. We will never know, but it does make me pause and have compassion for this man who was the father I grew up with. I spoke to my mother about this idea that Dad might have been gay. She never responded or agreed, but I noticed a very curious look on her face.

My father spent the rest of his life locked in a mental ward. My mother, as his ever-faithful wife, continued to visit him weekly until the door to his prison cell of the mind was unlocked in death. He was freed from his demons on March 8, 1994.

Goodbye, Dad!

"If you're brave enough to say goodbye, life will reward you with a new hello."

— PAULO COELHO

As a kid, my friends would always ask if my father was sick. I didn't really know what to say because there was so much more going on. I would usually say it had to do with the war. Before he was permanently diagnosed, we still believed it was the drinking. The army used his stays as what I liken to a Hollywood Rehab. They would dry him out and send him home. Although he was better when he wasn't drinking, it was just a matter of time before the drama would return, the personalities would appear, and the nightmare would continue.

After my father received his final diagnosis, he was permanently committed to the mental ward in the Menlo Park Veterans Hospital. To tell you the truth, until today, I never really got in touch with my feelings of having my father permanently committed to a mental hospital. Previous to his commitment, he would have shorter stays at the hospital. Because he would behave so badly and be so out of control, they'd put him in lockdown. At the time, I wasn't sure what was happening. I just knew he was crazy. We would go visit him until he was himself again. I remembered sitting in the lobby and doing my homework. Every once in a while, the doctors thought it would be good for me to see him so they'd bring me to a sliding window; the kind you see in movies when someone is visiting someone in prison.

One time my father had an unusually long stay at the Martinez Veterans Hospital and I had this idea of putting on a talent show for the veterans in the hospital. I believe I was also thinking of how I could make lemonade out of lemons, to make normal out of abnormal. It was my way of being in charge. Sure enough, I got some kids from St. David's and we put on a show.

Even after everything my mother endured throughout her marriage, she visited him every Sunday for at least ten years. She would bring him cigarettes, money for coffee, and snacks from the store. These visits could be compared to visiting someone who was incarcerated. Although I did feel sympathy for a man who was not only a prisoner of a mental ward, but a prisoner in his own mind and body, I didn't understand my mother's commitment to him. I find it somewhat questionable. What was this fifty plus year attachment to this man who caused so much tragedy in her life? After the torture chamber known as her marriage, she still felt the need to take care of him. She never explained it to me. Some things will always remain a mystery.

I recall some of my visits to see my father. I lived in Los Angeles at the time, so when I visited my mother, I would go with her to see him. It was about an hour or so drive. I didn't really want to go but I always felt it was my duty to accompany her. Multiple times during these visits, my father would blink his eyes like Jeannie in the 1960s TV show, *I Dream of Jeannie*. I think this was his way of thinking he was manifesting something. He would use this technique to pretend to give us money or some gift. Of course nothing ever appeared, but we played along, trying to lighten up the situation. On one particular day, he called after us, "*Don't forget to look in the trunk of the car. There's money for you in there for sure. I know how you both like money!"*

I remember going out to the car with my mother and pausing to look at each other before opening the trunk. Dad was so convincing that we just had to look. Naturally, nothing was there. We had a good laugh at ourselves.

After Dad's final diagnosis, the doctors let us know if he went out again, meaning if his unhealthy personality became dominant, that he might never come back. I was in my thirties the last time I saw my father. He was in the infirmary at the mental hospital. Because he was having some problems with his lungs, he was in a private room. He was a very heavy smoker and was suffering the health repercussions as a result. That day, he seemed a bit irritated, and the nurse confirmed that he had been agitated most of the day. In his room, I fell back into a very old habit and tried to calm him down and appease him like I trained myself to do as a young boy. He struck out at me violently, startling me. I was triggered and I catapulted back into my young childhood fear. It ran through my entire being and every fiber in my body. As I stepped back into safety, I looked at my mother, and then I looked straight into father's eyes. I made sure he could see me. I wasn't angry. I was just very clear. Emphatically and with a final commitment, I said, *"You will never scare me again Dad, I am through. Goodbye Dad."*

I didn't wait for his reply. I turned around and walked through those doors and I never looked back. I felt a sense of completion. It was emotional. I had tears in my eyes, but they were tears of power; the kind of power it takes to finally say, *"Enough is enough!"*

When my mother returned, I was having a cigarette outside of the facility. I let her know I would never return to see him again. I don't remember her reply. My father died a few years later. I never regretted walking out of his room and never seeing him again. I had finally protected my inner child. That moment was long overdue.

It was as if the Universe was affirming my disconnection from my father. The day he died, my mother could not get in touch with me because I was at a conference and I did not check my messages. When I finally did, there were around thirty messages from my mother. They progressed from frantic to scared to angry. She did not know why I had not returned her call. I remember her last message, "*Well, I have done everything else on my own! Why should this be any different.*"

It was disconcerting that she would say that, given all the times I'd stood by her. When we finally spoke, I asked if she wanted me to come home and she said, "*No, I took care of everything. He's being cremated and buried this week.*" I was amazed at how fast it all happened. No obituary. It was just over. All the years of drama and terror had ended in one swift decision and action. I guess the closure for me was the day I walked out of his hospital room.

I was surprised when the nurses and staff of father's hospital requested that I conduct the memorial gathering for him. Maybe it was because they knew I was an actor and probably comfortable with public speaking. I agreed. The attendees of the memorial were the guys who had been with my father all those years he was in the mental hospital. I remember that day clearly and how calm I was in that atmosphere. It reminded me of a scene from the film, *One Flew Over the Cuckoo's Nest*, with Jack Nicholson. The staff were yelling a lot of interesting and sometimes crass and pornographic things about my father. I have to admit, I had unusual control of that unruly audience. Perhaps this was a foreshadowing of my future as a minister, or maybe I was

161

just well practiced from an early age. Again, it was hard to believe it was over. To be honest, both as a kid and an adult, I always thought my father would outlive us all.

This Property is Condemned; The Little Man Returns

> "Whoever, at any time, has undertaken to build a
> new heaven has found the strength for it in his own
> hell..."
>
> - NIETZSCHE

At fifty-two years old, I stood in front of the home of my childhood on San Pablo Avenue, Space 60, for the last time. It seemed dwarfed compared to the terror I experienced there. As I gazed at that double-wide mobile home, it seemed impossible that the horror story called my childhood could have been contained within those walls. Pictures of my father's rages, my brother terrorizing us, and the cops coming in the middle of the night flashed before my eyes. From ages five through nineteen I discovered how to navigate and still remain sane through the terror we called crazy.

Why was I there now? The city of San Pablo was getting ready to demolish the trailer park that contained my childhood home and the trailer my mother lived in for almost fifty years. The owners told the tenants they were building new fabricated homes to relocate the people in the park. They claimed it would be a modern and safe place for residents to live. That would have been great for my mother. Thankfully I found out from an inside source that this was not going to happen. It was a lie. Instead, it would become the place where the San Pablo City Hall and government buildings are now located. The owners bought my mother out for a very small amount of money compared to the $400 a month she had paid for that space all those years. Where would she find a rent like that in 2008? I knew we would have to find a solution.

Mom was in her late eighties. I wished I had been wealthy and could really have helped her in those last years of her life. However, she was in much better financial shape than I was at that time. Fortunately, she had benefits from the government, social security, and a pension that would allow her to live modestly. Together, we discussed what would come next. There were really only two choices left for her. She would either stay in San Pablo in a small apartment or move to Los Angeles where my wife Rita and I lived. My mother did not want to leave her beloved Bay Area. And yet, she understood that she would need to be close to us. She'd already had a few emergency health challenges that had sent me driving to the Bay Area from Los Angeles in a hurry. When she said yes to moving to Los Angeles, I felt a drop in my stomach. My instinct told me things would never be the same for me or my mother.

As the workings of the Universe are perfect, as soon as the decision was made, an apartment opened up in our building in Los Angeles. Quite honestly, it was definitely a little too close for mother and son in my mind, but it was inevitable. Even as I write these words about what I call "The Big Move," I can feel triggers of anxiety in my body. We secured the apartment for her, and life was now taking an unexpected turn for us all. Although I didn't know it at the time, with "The Big Move" would come the biggest change in me that would affect our mother and son relationship forever.

We had not lived near one another for almost thirty-five years. I was always proud that my mother was an independent woman who could take care of herself. No child wants to see their parents get old; plus my fear was coupled with our relationship history. I felt like I was returning to my childhood. I was my mother's protector and now I would have to reclaim that position.

My father and brother had died one year apart from each other in 1994 and 1995. They were no longer present to terrorize us but how would we live and react to each other now? Although she would be safe, I knew she would not be happy living in Los Angeles. She was moving to be closer to me, but I felt like I was moving back home in my fifties and it did not feel good. Of course I know all about the circle of life and how it was my turn to take care of my mother. It was my duty as her son. I was all my mother had. As an adult I understood all of this and wanted to assist her, but my inner child was screaming at the top of his lungs, *"I haven't had my turn yet! What about me? I already did this!"*

As I stood in front of that trailer, these were some of the thoughts going through my head. The day had come to start the move. My mother would be letting go of a life of almost fifty years, and I would be coming back to a past I thought was over. As I flew to the Bay Area to help her move to her next chapter, I knew it would also be a new one for Rita and me.

As I entered the trailer, I was met by an unhappy surprise. My mother had promised me she would get some help to start the move and be at least half ready to go. I was appalled and shocked to find everything was still there. Although the place was clean, nothing had been packed or thrown out. The movers were coming in a few days. Taking care of fifty years of her possessions landed on my shoulders heavily.

My reaction was less than compassionate. I could feel my emotions swirling. All my childhood triggers went off. The pressure to make things right felt so intense, and yet my resentment was front and center. She, on the other hand, seemed quite untroubled by the task ahead and had made plans for us to go to the local fish fry at the Moose Lodge. I let her know I would not be going, and she left me alone with my past. In a way it was a blessing as it left me time to sort out my feelings. But there was no time for that. My job was to get her moved; not to feel like a victim.

I remember many meltdowns during the packing and preparation to move her. I still don't know how such a small double-wide trailer could hold all of that. Every drawer was stuffed, the walk-in closets were filled, and there was paperwork she'd kept from the 1960s, including her paystubs from forty years ago. There were endless piles of my father's army papers and hundreds of pictures. I felt like I was drowning in a sea of paper. As I sat with a glass or two of wine in the middle of this mess, crying and feeling lost, alone, and angry, I recall making many calls to Rita asking for Spiritual Mind Treatment (our form of affirmative prayer). My inner child was finally having that temper tantrum I never allowed him to have as a child.

As I write this, I admit I feel a sense of guilt that I was not considering how hard this must have been for my mother. There was a mental and emotional battle going on between my own feelings and the feelings of a little boy who wanted to make his mommy happy. The other part of me was screaming, "*You left me with all this to do. It's too much! You promised me you were going to pack and be ready for me. You broke your promise to me, again!*"

Broken promises were most definitely the trigger for me. The flood of good intentions and broken promises of my childhood inundated my mind. What was stirring such emotion? To be completely honest, I am just now discovering this as I write this part of the story. My emotions were being fanned by the rush to get the job done, while at the same time ignoring the pain and scars of the very long novel of my family history. My mind was thinking *"Get the job done! Don't feel what you are feeling!"*

I felt I was left all alone to complete the enormous task in front of me. Because of this, I was simply not listening to my deep inner voice telling me the hardest part of this move for me was not being able to take away my mother's pain. It angered me that I still felt I had to take on this childhood role in my fifties, while my mother was in a world of denial about leaving the Bay Area. I knew how hard this was for her, but she was using her lifelong coping skills of shutting down to get through life's challenges.

There were moments of looking at the bright side. My mother had not died. She was moving to her next life here on earth. This was an opportunity to let go of the old and start new, even at eighty-five years old. As the packing continued, my mother was obstinate. She did not want to let go or give away anything. We were constantly bickering and she would usually win. Why? Because I wanted to make her happy. I had always been her therapist throughout our life together. I knew the psychological reasons for her not wanting to let go of her stuff was because it would mean letting go of her home, friends, and all her memories. Hiding her emotions was her coping mechanism, not just during life with my father, but other times too. She always bragged about giving birth to me and never making a peep while the women around her were screaming and wrenching in pain. She let me know she would never let on that she was suffering. This badge of silence continued through her life. I wonder now if maybe my mother did not feel she deserved to scream out in pain. I thought I knew her so well but sometimes I question if I really knew her fully. Do we ever really know what is going on in another person's mind? I must say, I knew more about her feelings than most kids might know about their parents. It was my job to know, and now, I was stuck between the little boy who wanted to run away and cry and the Little Man who knew, practically speaking, he had little time to get her packed and moved.

When I was able to let go of my own resentment, I tried to find ways to let her talk about her feelings, but she was too shutdown. I've heard that when older people are urged to throw the clutter of their lives out, it stirs up the feelings of death being imminent. I'm not sure if this was the case with my mother, and really, I had no time to be her therapist. I was too preoccupied with the immense task in front of me of physically moving her out of her home. I had plenty of feelings too. However, they'd have to wait until later.

I did feel like a part of me was dying too. The memories of fear, terror, and the wonderful memories as well, were about to be emptied and demolished. I wondered if all the secrets of dark bedrooms and years of confusion could be demolished as well. As we continued to gather the few things we would rearrange in her new home in Los Angeles, it felt like a slow death for both of us.

There were a few humorous moments when a glass of wine helped us to wash down all those memories. There were goodbye parties at the Moose Lodge. (My mother was a member of the Loyal Order of Moose). I could tell by their talk and sharing that her friends were really going to miss her. Although we all knew it was the right thing to do, I wonder if everyone felt their own mortality through my mother.

It continued to be a terribly slow process. Finally, I was able to enlist the help of a few of her younger seventy-something friends who could help me dump the stuff we were throwing away and take other things to Goodwill. The moving day arrived. Ironically, the movers were ready to do the packing that I'd already done. As she had already paid them, I'm sure they were pleased. Now they would just have to pack a few loose items, her clothes, and the few pieces of furniture. We were complete.

As the truck pulled away from the house, we stood together and watched as what was left of fifty years of her life disappear from view. She did not make a sound; not a tear was shed and not a word passed between us. We walked back into the trailer and my mother took a seat in the middle of the living room on the one piece of furniture left – an outdoor plastic chair. As she sat there stoically, I felt a wave of emotions from pity to relief. The representative from the trailer park arrived for the last inspection. He was satisfied and handed her the final payoff check. It was time to leave. We made our way out to the new car she had purchased with the first check she'd received for initially signing the termination papers. Before getting in the car, my mother stood and looked at the trailer. The front porch had collapsed from the movement of the heavy furniture. That front porch held the memory of many nights of escape from my father's rages. Again, no words were spoken between us. We merely got in the car and drove away. Little did we know that this would be the last time my mother would ever see her beloved Bay Area.

As we silently bid farewell to the space on San Pablo Avenue, I remembered again that *wherever you go, there you are.* How much mental and emotional baggage would we bring to our new life together? We would soon find out. As we drove, our light chatter covered up the emotional silence, but there was no authenticity to it. We couldn't discuss what was really happening in the recesses of each of our minds. I tried to lighten things up, as I had always done throughout her life, but I just couldn't help her sadness. It didn't feel good at all.

I loved my mother's independence. I felt free knowing my mother could take care of herself. I remember being nineteen and leaving for Los Angeles. She was safe from my father and I could leave and claim some of my independence. On an intellectual level, I understand that what I was going through was a natural part of life between children and their aging parents. It's the circle of life after all. The only difference for me is I had already spent most of my young life as a caretaker. I want to be honest with my feelings and not disguise my words with what I believe a good boy would think and do in order to please the reader and my mother. I will do this even if it means taking on the societal role of being a bad boy.

My inner child was out in full force. It felt like I was taking a step backward in time. I was terrified of going back to the role of emotional caretaker, and now, physical caretaker. As we drove the last miles to Los Angeles on Interstate 5, the road my mother and I had taken so many times to visit each other, these were the thoughts that were crossing my mind. As we moved toward the last stretch that is known as the Grapevine, a new life was beginning for my mother, and for Rita and me as well. I was terrified.

Mom's New Life Becomes My Old Life

"Everything must change. Nothing stays the same.
Everyone must change. Nothing stays the same.
The young become the old,
Mysteries do unfold.
Cause that's the way of time
Nothing and no one goes unchanged."
- BERNARD IGHNER

We arrived in Los Angeles. Mom would stay with us for the night until her furniture came. The furniture did arrive the next morning and she seemed overly excited to get to her new home. I felt that independent side of her come out. Could this new arrangement work out? Would my independent mother find her place in Los Angeles even with her apartment right across the hall from us? I had not lived that close to my mother for over thirty years. The thoughts of freedom for both of us fled from my mind quickly.

I had to do what I could to make sure my mother was happy in her new life. I had to erase the pain and sadness she might be feeling leaving her beloved Bay Area. I wanted to know I could still make her laugh like I did all those years. What I would find out is that making her feel happy and fulfilled was a childhood illusion. In the meantime, I'd do my best to fulfill the role I created for myself. I'd build her life anew in LA. It was somewhat fun in the beginning. I told myself living in close proximity to each other gave me the opportunity to be around her during her golden years. Truly, that's what I wanted to believe. While she was still somewhat independent, it seemed possible.

Rita and I set out to make her feel at home. We decorated her veranda with plants. It would be a place where she could sit and we could all enjoy the evenings together. The veranda was large enough to share dinner and we did so on many occasions. My mother already knew a lot of people from our Center/Church and our life in LA because of all her previous visits. We created a housewarming party for her. It was well-attended and reflected the new life and home she would have in Los Angeles. Her biggest challenge would be driving. In the Bay Area, she never had a problem. She drove those highways easily and comfortably. She'd have to relearn the area. Would she be able to do it in her late eighties? It was a concern for Rita and me.

My mother worked out at the gym for most of her life. I know it was what kept her healthy enough to survive all the stress she experienced with my father. She was in excellent health and shape for a woman in her late eighties. She prided herself on being able to do one-hundred sit-ups — "*the real ones,*" she would brag. It made sense to continue her ability to exercise so I got her set up at the gym.

She couldn't go without Catholicism and her Sunday Mass. Fortunately, St. Charles Church was just down the street and easy to get to. At least to begin with, she would have no trouble driving herself there. We did our best to get her settled, and now it was time to move on with my and Rita's life. The only difference is it would become a blend of our life and my mother's. I'm going to be honest. I feel that it put a strain on our marriage. We had been married a short eight years. If you asked Rita, she would tell you that my mother coming to live with us was what she considered the end of the honeymoon stage. Could our relationship take this new experience? Time would tell and I knew we would do our best. I was grateful that our marriage relationship was solid. If it hadn't been, I don't think we would have survived this.

I was now dividing myself in two, all the time leaving a lot of me out of the equation. If Rita was frustrated, she did a good job concealing it. The gift for me was that she and my mother got along well and actually really liked one another. However, no matter how I looked at it, we were in a three-way relationship. It was not easy for Rita and I to move ahead with our lives. We were trying to create a future together and keep my mother's life intact at the same time. I do have to say, the three of us did a pretty damn good job creating good times out of a very complicated situation. One thing I made very clear to my mother from the beginning was that Rita came first. I would never make the mistake of putting my mother ahead of my relationship like I had done in the past. Although I was telling myself I was putting Rita first, I felt torn much of the time.

After two years, there was another move in store for the three of us. Rita and I had lived in our apartment for eleven years and now our intention was to move into a house. It took us a bit of time, but while I was traveling with my job, Mom and Rita found a house to rent that had a mother-in-law house in the back. This blessing helped us subsidize the move as my mother could help with the rent. We always made the best of a difficult situation.

The move was exciting for Rita and me. It was fun to look forward to living in a house after so many years of apartment living and growing up in a trailer. On the other hand, I don't think my mother was as happy as we were about the move. I believe she never got over having to leave her mobile home.

As I look back, I consider this move the beginning of the end for my mother. She was nearing ninety, and that in itself bothered her immensely. Up to this point, she never minded her birthdays. Now, when I excitedly mentioned her ninetieth birthday coming up, her reaction was almost hostile.

Her dependency on me seemed to be getting stronger too. It was time to get her driver's license renewed. Although she worked hard studying for the exam and passed it, she rarely left the house unless it was with us or one of her newly made friends. Our friends suggested I stop her from driving, but I could not do it. She finally stopped herself when she had a minor accident and her insurance skyrocketed. She came to her own conclusion that it would be cheaper not to drive anymore. I would become her full-time driver, cook, and entertainer. Here we were, back at the beginning.

A House Divided Against Itself!

"Leaving home in a sense involves a kind of second birth in which we give birth to ourselves."
— ROBERT NEELLY BELLAH

Mom's ninetieth birthday was approaching and she made it very clear she wasn't happy about it. In fact, she hated it when I mentioned it. Rita and I were planning a big surprise party that we hoped would cheer her up. I believe she thought ninety was the age that made her old. She never said that, but as you know by now, I was pretty good at reading her. You might say with some resignation, *"Well, it's natural her health should decline; she was ninety years old after all."* My belief system tells me that your emotional attitudes play a great part in your physical health.

From her ninetieth birthday onward, she began a most definite decline in her physical, emotional, and mental health. She started to have episodes of illness that needed medical treatment. It was all about her heart. On one particular occasion, we thought we were going to lose her for sure. The doctor told me she would most definitely not make it. I remember we had a beautiful last moment together in the hospital. She let me know how much I had meant to her. She told me, for the first time, she appreciated how I had taken such good care of her. She verbalized my childhood sacrifice and also told me she wished it had been different.

If that had been our final goodbye, it would have been the perfect movie ending. However, she wouldn't be leaving us for quite a while. She pulled through and was released to go home.

Thus began the continuous health episodes that put her in and out of rehabilitation homes. At the same time, I was going back to school in my fifties to complete my psychology degree while at the same time getting my ministerial license. Compounding this, we were suffering from financial instability, and I was balancing my life between taking care of my mother and wanting to nurture my relationship with Rita. I could feel myself slowly slipping from the Little Man of the past who had to take care of his mother and keep her safe to the adult man who was feeling a sense of resentment. I was resenting the fact that I could not make her young and independent again. I resented that I felt I was back in the past doing what I did as a young boy. To top it off, I felt guilty for feeling that way. There was a daily tug-of-war taking place within me between my life and my need to save and take care of my mother.

Rita's plate was as full as mine. She did the best she could to help, especially when I was out of town working. We were grateful for our friends who rallied around us in support. They loved Rita and I so much that they went out of their way to help. I remember many meltdowns during this period similar to those of my childhood. Every time there was a major event during that period – my graduation, ministerial panels, and finally our long overdue honeymoon, my mother would have some sort of physical crisis. A part of me felt like it was purposeful on her part. This might have been unconscious in her mind but I know how powerful the subconscious is.

My mother could always find a way to get to her son. We

had mutually established a new relationship that I would be there for her during this new phase of her journey. My obsession with making her happy included trips to Taco Bell to bring home her favorite treat and making homemade mashed potatoes for her every night. One time, when she mentioned a new kind of banana flavored Cheerios, I wanted to surprise her and I went to the supermarket to find them.

As I looked at the many types of Cheerios, and saw there were no banana flavored ones, I remember starting to panic, almost starting to cry at the thought of not being able to purchase them. I called her in an emotional fit, *"Mom, they don't have the new flavored Cheerios. I can't find them. I can't find them!"*

I was having a meltdown in the cereal aisle at Ralph's Supermarket. She said calmly, *"Honey, I just mentioned they had a new flavor. It is not that important."*

In October 2012, I had just received my Bachelor's Degree in Psychology and had already passed my ministerial test and panels. We had worked out an amazing, affordable trip to Kaua`i. It was a long overdue honeymoon and a celebration for my accomplishments. As we neared the time to go, my mother was in physical rehab again. We felt it was actually a good time to go since she was safe and cared for by professionals. We had the support of friends who would go visit her while we were away. At the same time, Rita and I were already planning what we were going to do with our ministerial licenses. We had decided we were going to start our own new work within the guidelines of Centers for Spiritual Living. The only question was where and when.

The vacation to Kaua`i would answer the question of where we would start this new work. The only question was when. We decided not to say anything to anyone until we had made more plans. Those plans disintegrated the moment we got back to the mainland, when our Spiritual Leader, James Mellon, said, "*So, when are you moving to Kaua`i?*"

We were most definitely called to this new life. I knew it was the right thing to do, and yet it was clouded by the thought of telling my mother. We knew we would be bringing her with us, as difficult as that might be. I remember the day I told her that we had decided to move and start a Center in Kaua`i. My mother loved Hawai`i and had taken almost twenty trips there. I was hoping she would be thrilled, but this was definitely not a happy moment for her. It was strange how it unfolded. I told her that we were moving and she immediately said, "*NO! You are not moving anywhere.*"

It was definitely clear to her that I was not going to do that. She would have no part of this new plan. I felt like a little boy being scolded. I most definitely did not have her permission. In that moment, I was frozen in time and space. I knew I was not a little boy, and yet I felt like she had that parental power over me. I compared it to wanting to have something as a kid and knowing I had to convince her in order to get it. I immediately backed off. I told her it was not happening now and that we would talk about it later. It was obvious that she needed some time to digest the reality of what I told her. I would start to work out the details anyway.

I started looking for assisted living places on Kaua`i. Many of our "well-meaning" acquaintances who were deeply involved in my mother's life began to voice their opinions both to her and to us. I began to give my power away to these people. My guilt was over shadowing my decision-making abilities. To say I felt overwhelmed would be an understatement. However, I pushed through my guilt and we continued with our plan.

Rita had a full-time position and I was working a series of independent jobs. We decided this was reason enough for me to go to Kaua`i first. I would begin to plant seeds and start this new venture. A subtle fear began working beneath the surface of our lives as we headed toward my departure date in March. We got through the holidays, trying to enjoy them, but an impending doom was hovering in my mind. It was the fear of me leaving my mother. You see, those well-meaning acquaintances had somehow convinced her that it wasn't a good idea for her to go with us. She was easily swayed. She told us that she didn't think it was good for her to make this kind of change at her age. Was she testing me? Maybe. Later, she would tell me she didn't really think I would go.

As I look back, I wonder if we should have forced her to go, but instead we began to look for an assisted living place in Los Angeles. The amount of stress I felt while planning to make this move was overwhelming. First of all, we had little money, and when I say *little money*, I mean it.

Even with the financial facts in our face, I knew this was the right move to make. It was even more than following a calling. I believe it had a higher meaning. I believe there was a deep karmic separation taking place between my mother and me. As I pointed out before, if she had died that time in the hospital, we might have had that Hollywood ending. She didn't, and we would not.

As my mother's fear of me leaving her grew stronger, we began to argue more. I would have meltdowns caused by my inner guilt and shame that were intense. How could I leave my mother at this critical time? I know many people who would have never done what I was about to do. We continued to argue back and forth about her coming with us. In the deepest part of me, I knew this journey was not hers to take. Even after everything we had been through together, this was the darkest time in our relationship. There was no way to get past the feeling that I was abandoning her. I had to admit, in reality, that was just what I was doing. Yet I question whose reality was more important to fulfill. If I did not believe in the deepest part of me that it had to be done, I would have never have put either of us through this.

This time in my life should have felt like a great adventure to be relished and enjoyed even if it was a frightening jump into the great unknown. However, as the time got closer to making that jump, it felt more like a time of gut-wrenching agony on my psyche. I realized that the anger that I felt and projected on my mother was a guilt I could not yet release. As I look back on it now, my biggest regret is that I was not able to experience this new adventure packed with joy. Instead, it was filled with gloom.

Here was the Little Man trapped back in his past. The Little Man who would have always put his mother first was now taking a leap for himself. Although he would make every attempt to make sure she was taken care of, it would never be enough for him, or for her. How could it be enough when she was not getting her way with the boy who would have at one time given his life and much of his mental energy up to make sure she was happy. I was catapulted back to the time when I was fourteen. I had experienced a terrible car accident and felt myself flying out of my body. I was most definitely going to die. I knew it. However, I distinctly remember making the decision to come back to my body because I knew my mom couldn't handle it. How would she survive without me?

I have heard that when a woman is in labor there is a time called "transition." It is right in the last moments while the baby is crowning where the mother is willing to let go of her own life for the child. Either the mom or the baby will survive. At this time, I felt it was either her or me. I knew I would not survive if I did not allow myself to be born anew and leave the womb/home of my mother. It may sound dramatic, but reader, it was. I was so emotionally torn. At one point at a party when I was expressing my stress and feeling of victimhood to a friend, she said something about my mother needing me. I was so triggered by her comment that I exploded at her, *"All I know is that it is either her or me at this point because I am breaking."*

I can remember the look on this "not so well-meaning" friend's face. She acted like I was going to kill her. *"What did you say?"* she questioned me.

"It's a fucking metaphor," I screamed. *"Can't you see I can't take the guilt of constantly being pulled at by my mom?"* I'm not sure she understood or wanted to. She had her judgments.

As it got closer to the time of my departure, my mother started to become angrier at me. On numerous occasions she would say, *"I never thought you would do this to me, I never thought you would turn on me like this."*

I know that through my younger years, she was used to me doing exactly what she wanted. But as I got older, she had gotten used to me doing exactly what I wanted. Really, she had taught me that kind of independence. It was a contradiction. When I did do what I wanted, she would threaten me by saying she would not have anything to do with me. It always surprised me given that my father and brother Danny tortured her for years. How could my simple decisions that didn't agree with her stir up so much anger in her?

During my early twenties, when I called off my Dynasty wedding eight weeks before the date, my mother was very supportive and helped me through a difficult time. After it was all done and my fiancé and I were going our separate ways, my mother informed me she had planned to have nothing to do with me after I was married. Her excuse was she felt my fiancé did not like her. "*I didn't tell you before your marriage because I didn't want to get in the middle of your relationship.*"

She might have felt that at the time, but she ended up being close friends with both my fiancé and her family until her death. More contradictions. I am expressing this to make it clear that whether you consider me leaving my mother at this time in her life was right or wrong, it wasn't until this point that I truly discovered the dysfunction in our relationship. Although I try my best to understand all of our feelings — my mother's, mine, and Rita's — I still believe that as difficult as this was on all of us, in the end, it would turn out to be a healthy move. The history between my mom and me was coming to an end. It was time to finally move on.

The day for me to leave for Kaua'i arrived at last. My colleagues, mentor, and friends gave me a big going away party at the NoHo Arts Center for New Thought. The theme, of course, was Hawai`i. It is a blurry memory except that I do remember shutting down a lot of my emotions to protect myself from the incredible guilt I was experiencing. Here I was getting ready for the biggest and most glorious time of my life. This was a time that needed all my strength and confidence. I was taking off by myself to start a new life, plant seeds for our new work, and build and grow Center for Spiritual Living Kaua'i. Instead, I felt I was walking to my guillotine. It was supposed to be a time of celebration but I felt as though I was killing my mother with my decision. I remember being in the air on Hawaiian Airlines getting ready for the final descent into Kaua`i. My mind was screaming,

"Please, let's just keep circling!" I was scared. I did not have my usual confidence in my ability to experience change. At the same time, there was a sense of relief to finally be on the island. I began to let go of the breath that I had been holding for the past six months. Ready or not, I was here and it was time to get moving. I made my way to my sublet house in Kapahi and my adventure began.

Right now, I will take a pause and give Rita and me a whole lot of credit for taking on such a big project by ourselves. We only knew one person on the island and here I was, ready to share a philosophy that no one knew anything about. Please note that this ability to jump into the unknown was backed by a principle we had become well acquainted with and had practiced for almost twenty years. We knew our heartfelt, powerful decision would be met with the Power of the Law of Cause and Effect. What we had put out in consciousness would lead the way to our success.

In Los Angeles, Rita had begun the process of looking for an assisted living home for Mom, in addition to working fulltime and breaking down a house and the life we had built over the last fourteen years. On my end, I was meeting people, opening up business accounts for CSL Kaua'i, and trying my best to have something ready for Rita's arrival in May. Even with the sense of excitement I felt at this new beginning, my phone calls to my mother were less than encouraging. She was terribly unhappy and downright pissed off. I had developed a sense of guilt now for both my mother and Rita. I felt the immense weight of leaving my mother and for being the one who was living in paradise while Rita had her hands full. I remember my phone calls with Rita and not wanting to talk about the beautiful beaches too much because I felt it would make her sad. Instead I focused on my guilt about Mom and the negative aspects of what was happening. You see, no matter where you go, there you are. I had most definitely brought my unfinished baggage with me to paradise.

Rita did find a place for Mom that met the limited budget she had for rental. My lease in Kapahi had run out and I was in search of a new place to rent on the island. That place would be in Princeville with a wonderful woman and her husband on their property. It was a lovely one room bungalow. I would joke with Rita on the phone that I was the pool boy without the pool. My state of mind was not in the best place. I couldn't release my guilt and I felt like I was crumbling under the financial strain. I remember thinking continually, "*I need a break, please!*"

The Fall of Princeville

"Paradise is not a place, it's a state of mind."
                                    - FRANK SONNENBERG

That break would come the day after my birthday on May 2, 2013. Rita put some money in our Hawai`i account so I could have a steak for my birthday and we zoomed for a candlelight dinner together. It was wonderful. The next morning I woke up in a very foul mood. I felt desperate for relief of any kind. I had my coffee and left the bungalow for my daily run on the Princeville path. Running had always been a great stress reliever for me, and this time would be no different. Before I left, I made my daily morning call to Rita. She knew my state of mind was not good. Yes, I was frustrated and angry. I screamed out to her, *"I just need a fucking break!"* Later, she told me she had a foreboding feeling after that call.

"Ask and you shall receive." As I ran, my feelings of desperateness and anger seemed to expand. I turned around on the path to run back. I tried to calm myself with positive affirmations to release the negativity I was feeling. This is what we call *spiritual bypassing*. I wasn't dealing with my feelings; just trying to cover them up. Perhaps, if I had sat and quietly meditated and contemplated for a moment, what happened next might have never happened. As the affirmations were pouring out of my mouth, I flew through the air and onto the ground. I had tripped on a root. I landed hard. I could not get up or move my arm. I knew I was in trouble and the

pain was excruciating. I had left my phone at the bungalow. Suddenly, a woman appeared to help me. She just happened to be a nurse and she had a phone. The only number I could remember was Rita's. The Princeville security guard, who could have played Barney Fife on *The Andy Griffith Show*, appeared and called an ambulance. I couldn't remember the name of my street and just kept mouthing the words, "*Liho, Liho,*" through my tears.

"*Man down, man down and delirious,*" was the security guard's message to 911.

Oh my God, this cannot be happening. The ambulance came and off I went for an hour-long bumpy ride to the hospital. All I could think was, "*I have no time for this!*" The paramedics kept giving me morphine. I heard them talking to the doctors on the phone, "*I gave him such and such amount and he's still in pain.*"

I heard the doctor on the other end saying, "*Just give him more!*" They didn't know I have the pain threshold of an elephant.

Upon arriving at the hospital, the x-ray confirmed it. I had a fractured shoulder. I got the break I wanted, or thought I needed. The doctor called it a "perfect break" because it wouldn't require surgery. Fortunately, I had already met some very wonderful people on the island. As it often does on Kaua'i, it didn't take long before the coconut wireless was set in motion. They all came to my rescue at the hospital.

Back on the Mainland Rita was going crazy, not knowing what my condition was or how to get any information about me. She decided not to call my mother until she heard from the hospital or my friends. My mother just happened to call my bungalow to talk to me. My landlord answered the phone. Thinking it would be good to tell her, he informed her I was on my way to the hospital. I can only imagine her reaction. If you remember, she had always admonished me not to get hurt as a child. Rita later told me she called her, screaming, "*What happened to my boy? What happened to my boy???*"

A more than profound thing occurred the day of the accident which I know was no accident. I was alone. I couldn't drive. I had become dependent on everyone around me. This was the moment I could have gone home to take a breather, to calm my mother down, to rest from my intense emotional strain. Rita asked me, "*Do you want to come home earlier than we intended and then we can go back together?*"

"*No,*" I answered firmly. "*I am home.*"

Although I was still feeling guilty and my emotional and physical conditions had not changed, I realized I was home. I believe when Rita asked me that question was the day I finally truly moved to Kaua`i. Although I did go back to help with the finalizing of our move and to move my mother to her new home, our new life had truly begun. I went back to LA at the end of the month to finalize our relocation. My arm was in a sling. My mother was very unhappy. Moving her to a smaller place was similar to the move from the Bay Area. She resisted. I felt like I was taking things away from her as we let go of pieces of furniture we knew wouldn't fit into her new home.

As for Rita and I, we were moving on Memorial Day weekend and leaving to start our life together and open CSL Kaua'i. We were able to fit everything we were taking with us into a four -by-four foot crate. Our treasures were mostly comprised of books and a few keepsakes. The hardest part of letting go for me was going through all those pictures. There were thousands and thousands of memories in albums. Time was running out, and our fellow minister who was helping us pack and discard things helped me to remember that those photos were my past and I was starting anew.

Going over to my mother's new place to say goodbye was the hardest moment of my life because I knew she must have felt I was abandoning her. The Little Man who spent his entire life making her happy was walking out the door. At the last moment, I remembered her wanting a certain toilet paper and Alvera Kleenex (the ones that were soft and had lotion in them). In a frustrated tone, she asked if I could find the time to get them for her. Of course, they provided these things at the assisted living home but she wanted her special kind. I made sure to give her this last moment of taking care of her, just like I used to.

Rita and I were at a farewell meal at our friend and mentor's home. I'm sure there were other people there, but we were so emotionally drained, I don't remember who they were. After dinner, another friend picked us up to take us to a hotel near the airport because our plane was leaving very early in the morning. Rita was so tired she fell asleep in the car. The next day we woke up, and off we went to our island in the middle of the Pacific Ocean.

Opening and Closing Night!

> *"The closing of a door can bring blessed privacy and comfort - the opening, terror. Conversely, the closing of a door can be a sad and final thing - the opening a wonderfully joyous moment."*
>
> *-ANDY ROONEY*

Our new adventure was just beginning. Rita and I breathed life into our new home in the middle of the Pacific Ocean. Jane and Erick, the owners of the bungalow I was living in prior to Rita's arrival, gave us one month to be there together. They really enjoyed having me as a tenant but did not want two people in their bungalow. We begged for the extra month in order to secure another living space. They introduced us to Lilly, one of the most amazing people I'd met on the island so far. Lilly was just celebrating her ninetieth birthday. She had a home a couple of blocks away from the bungalow. She was leery to rent to us at first, but Jane vouched for us, even saying she would pay the rent if we somehow defaulted. Of course, we would never do that, but what a great gesture on her part. *"They can be trusted,"* she told Lilly, *"and if they don't pay their rent, I will pay it. That is how much I believe in them."*

I look back now and can see how much we were guided to be on Kaua`i and do the work we are doing now. Rita, who has more strength than anyone I have ever met, was determined to start our new work and the Center of Spiritual Living Kaua'i on July 7th,, 2013. We even made postcards with the date on them. We added, "*Location TBA. Call 808-755-9177 for more information.*" We couldn't announce where our first service would be because we had no idea where the location was. I suggested we wait until we did, but Rita wanted no part of it. "*If we announce it, we are letting the Universe know the time is now.*"

We thought that looking for a banquet room in a hotel would be the place to start our search.

FREEZE FRAME!!!!!!!! Where is my mother and how is she doing? The one thing I will always be grateful for is our friends who were also my mother's friends. They willingly volunteered to check in on her and continue to assist her if she needed something. I felt somewhat at peace, knowing Mom was safe in her new assisted living home. In a short time, I would find out that these friends had another intention for my mother and would undermine me. As I look back on this, I am not sorry I moved to Kaua'i but I am sorry I gave my mother over to people who I thought I could trust. I know they wanted to help, but I now apologize to these people for laying too much responsibility on them. At the time, I thought I was doing the best for my mother. Now I realize I was doing the best for me. I also regret that I did not force her to come with us, and instead allowed our so-called friends to convince her that it was better that she stayed in Los Angeles.

Closer to her death, Mom confided in me that the only thing she regretted was not coming to Hawai'i with us. It was a place she loved with all her heart. In hindsight, which never does us any good, I agree with her. It would have been better for her on so many levels. Yet, I believe things worked out exactly the way they should have. There are no mistakes. When I look at it from a more mature and less emotional perspective, I see that I could not have continued a relationship with her that was so locked in the past while at the same time starting a new life. The Little Man, who was still determined to make her happy and give her what she wanted at his expense, had to grow up!

As Rita and I began to put our new life together and build a new spiritual community, introducing Science of Mind to an island that did not know of this teaching, my mother continued to show her displeasure. It wasn't the small room she was forced to live in that upset her. She liked small places. She had friends who helped her, visited her, and took her out. I am sure her anger was two-fold. I had deserted her and she had lost her independence; an independence which she had fought for and won most of her life.

If she were here now, I would say, *"I am sorry Mom that you had to start over again as you had done so many times in your life as an army wife. You loved it then, but now, in the end, it was not as easy, was it Mom?"*

My mother had a stubborn streak that didn't help bring peace to this situation. I called her several times a day which kept me plugged into my guilt perfectly. At first, she showed her disdain for my actions by refusing to participate in any of the many wonderful activities at the assisted living. She would let me know I was not the boss of her life. I will admit that it was taking a toll on me. However, the building of the new Center helped me to lessen my focus on my mother's displeasure. It was more exciting to plow the fertile ground of our new life. We were on a mission to succeed.

I always considered it a weakness on my part to leave my mother. However, I now see from the perspective of my own personal growth how instrumental my mother's role was in building this Center. I see, for the first time, what strength it took to leave her and that it was that very strength that was required to build CSL Kaua'i.

Finally, I think Mom got bored with the idea that I might return to California to be by her side. She slowly began to join the activities at her new assisted living home. She even befriended people. For a moment, she seemed happy and became that familiar mother of my past. With the change in her attitude, she also began to become more interested in what I was doing on Kaua`i. The humor that was such a big part of our relationship seemed to return.

Rita and I fulfilled our intention and opened the doors of CSL Kaua`i on July 7th, 2013. We continued the walk that we now liken to walking the Camino de Santiago. We were still struggling financially, but we were never poor. Our spirits were high and we were filled with energy and love for the new life we were building.

It was just before Christmas when I managed to make a trip back to California to see Mom. We had a good time but there was a heavy feeling lurking at the heart of our visit. For me, it felt like the feeling you have when you've broken up with someone and yet try to remain friends. It feels weird using this metaphor, but I know it was the truth of our relationship. While I was there we had a few nice talks. She let me know she had been told that I was happy doing what I was doing. She said she realized that since I was happy, it was for the best that I had moved. I could tell she meant it, and yet her spirit appeared broken. Strangely, I do not recall everything about that trip. This is unusual for me because I usually remember everything in detail. I think it was most likely because I was very cut off emotionally and my guilt still lingered. I remained that confused Little Man who had left his mama, the Little Man who could not take away his mommy's pain. While I was with her, we numbed our feelings by going out, including several Christmas parties and lunches with friends. In spite of everything she might have been feeling, her generosity for taking others out and her love of restaurants had not changed. Soon it was time for me to leave and go back to Kaua`i. As I review all of this, I remember my mother telling me about her early life when she would leave her mother after a visit. Her mother would be so distraught every time that finally she told her, "*Mom, I am not going to come visit you anymore if you are going to be so upset every time I leave.*"

It seems life repeats itself. I did indeed leave my mother with all of her feelings. It wasn't easy to know exactly what those feelings were, but I knew I was the cause. I returned to Kaua`i and continued my work building the Center and my daily phone calls to my mother. I also continued my almost daily correspondence with her friends who helped me keep track of how she was doing. As the months went on, her body continued to break down. She had what the doctor called mild strokes and her heart issues continued, along with mild dementia. She would call me in the middle of the night and wonder why they were not serving breakfast. She told me she was dressed and waiting in the dining room. I would tell her to go back to her room. These episodes were compounded by urinary infections that made her appear mentally out of control. Although the doctors told me these things were all normal at her age, it didn't stop me from being worried. I spoke with her medical care team and I decided to fly out to assess her and the situation. It was the end of June 2014.

When I arrived, my mother was at the hospital. She was so happy to see me, even with my long hair. Note that my hair was always a point of contention between us. She hated long hair on men, especially me. When she told me my hair was beautiful, I knew she was really happy to see me.

Elaine, whom she called her best friend, was in the room when I arrived. They had a very special bond and I considered Elaine family. However, her willing acceptance of being my mother's caretaker in my absence put a strain on our friendship and that friendship would finally be destroyed.

I was severely judged by many people during this time. However, what I know is that they only had snapshots of my life based on the last two years. They saw me as irresponsible, and yet they had no idea of my fifty-five years of being her caretaker. My mother seemed to forget this too. This trip, which would end up being my last, would turn out to be a bitter ending to our relationship. I was visiting my mother every day while talking to the doctors at the same time. One morning I had my usual stop off at Starbucks before going to the hospital to visit her and I got a call from her, "*Where are you?*" Her tone was so angry.

"*What's the matter Mom? I am on my way to see you now.*" I felt defensive.

"*You get your ass over here right now. I am not putting up with this anymore,*" was her reply.

Even as I write this, I can feel it is happening all over again and I feel angry and hurt. I got to the hospital and she was still angry and cold. "*How dare you come here and not stay with me.*"

Did she think I should not see anyone else while I was there and actually sleep at the hospital? From that moment and for the rest of my trip, it seemed to get worse. Her contempt for me grew even stronger. It was quite a rollercoaster ride. When Elaine was visiting, Mom would ignore me like a child trying to make me jealous. The subtext was, "*I like her better than you.*" She glared at me with what felt like deep hatred. I knew this couldn't be true. It was my mother after all, but I had no sign that she felt otherwise.

Finally, the doctors said she could not stay in the hospital any longer. There was nothing more they could do for her. Hospitals are not hotels, and although my mother preferred to be there rather than in the rehabilitation center, it was not an option. The moment any crisis is over, the hospital discharges you. If you cannot care for yourself, you end up in a rehabilitation center.

Mom was sent to a rehab center because she was not fit enough to be back in her assisted living home. She had been in this particular place several times before and she hated it there. I will admit it was not the highest of vibrations, but I was not able to save her. Home care was just impossible financially.

Oftentimes in these centers, the staff are overworked and not very congenial. Some patients have been there for a long time and are not very happy. Yes, it was a depressing energy. I was very sad she had to be in such a place and the Little Man in me was sure he was responsible for getting her out of there. I decided I would find a way to do just that. I went to her assisted living to get some of her clothes and bring them to her. She was not happy at all and was not obeying the rules of rehab therapy. There was a woman in the next bed who was a character. She seemed to take a dislike to me immediately. She would eavesdrop on our conversations. She pretended to like me and spoke of her time in Hawai`i and wanted to know about our new Center. Then, I would hear her on the phone talking about me. I was the horrible negligent son. I finally pulled the curtain between her bed and my mother's. I told her I could hear her and actually told her to knock it off.

I did not want to see my mother die in a place like this and yet she seemed to be heading that way. I was trying to get options for her care but sometimes working through the medical system is like being on a hamster's wheel. The rehab center told me if she turned in all her monthly benefits to them, they could keep her permanently. That was not going to happen on my watch. Mom kept trying to be civil to me but the strain was still there. There was nothing I could do — on so many levels. One afternoon, we were pretending to have a conversation and she looked at me and said, "*You know I was thinking that maybe God took the wrong son when he took Danny.*"

As you already know, my brother Danny had been killed by a car as he walked on to a median in the streets of San Francisco. When she said this, I was stunned. Did I hear her wrong? "*What?*" I asked her again.

Calmly she said, "*I just was wondering if God took the wrong son and should have taken you.*"

I could not believe my ears or my mouth. My brother who had caused her decades of heartbreak, chaos, and pain should have been spared and I should have taken his place? I exploded like a volcano. "*How dare you! After everything I have done for you my whole life!*"

The neighbor in the next bed tried to interfere. I told her to shut up. I had never been that hurt or angry in my life. Just then Elaine showed up. We stepped out of the room together and I told her what Mom had said. I was literally sobbing. All Elaine said was, "*She wants her way. You know your mom. This is her last try at getting you to come back. You know Katie is very manipulative.*"

I was surprised at her comment. After all, Mom was sure Elaine was her best friend. Elaine went back into the room while I took a walk. I felt like a trapped and wounded animal. To this day, I still work on releasing the hurt from her words, telling myself that her fear of being alone and losing me caused her to make one last attempt to awaken my guilt and get me to stay. When I went back into the room, she tried to backpedal as she did so many times when she had spoken harsh words to me. Maybe Elaine had talked to her. I can't remember what she said because I was totally shutdown. I left for the night and told her I would come back tomorrow. I really wondered whether I would go back. I needed to process this one for sure. I think I called Rita to debrief and receive a Spiritual Mind Treatment, but I'm not certain.

The next day, of course, I did return. I continued my quest to help my mother. I never mentioned what she had said to me again and it was swept under the carpet with so much of our past that was left unspoken. I felt quite defeated and alone. In the meantime, another UTI was brewing on the horizon and she was taken back to the hospital. (A special note: not only does a UTI interfere with your mental faculties but it can give one the strength of a superhero.) When I got to the hospital, I was met by an angry, delusional woman. She continued yelling at me and calling me names. The hospital gave her something to calm her down. I followed her gurney as they took her down in the basement to run some tests. It was so cold down there. Anyone who knows my mother knows she does not like the cold. I tried to get blankets to wrap her, but her only reply was, *"Leave me alone!"*

I reacted like a little boy who couldn't understand why his mommy was mad. I remember finally asking, *"Mom, why are you so mad at me?"*

As she looked at me with daggers in her eyes, she said, *"I never dreamed you could ever do this to me."* She just kept repeating it over and over. I tried to speak, even to make amends, but she was shutdown and closed off. I was exhausted. All I could do was surrender in silence.

After the tests, they wheeled her back to her room. It was very late. Her silence continued. I pulled out the couch bed in her room and went to sleep. The next morning, the antibiotics seemed to be taking effect. She was in better spirits, but still standoffish. I left to take a shower. *"I'll be back later,"* was all I could say.

When I came back they were taking her for more tests and physical therapy. I stood by her side and tried a little humor to lighten the moment. I said to the technicians and physical therapists, *"My mother is a super woman. She can do whatever you need her to do."*

She looked at me with disgust, *"You are so funny, you must be a comic. Do you get paid to be that funny?"*

I just made light of it and bowed out of the conversation. When we were alone later, I let her know that I was not going to be treated like this much longer and she needed to stop it. I was met with silence. The next day, she seemed to be getting better as the UTI had definitely subsided with the antibiotics. She was polite to me, but still cold. I was hoping I could get her back to her assisted living home. That was my goal because I was scheduled to leave in a few days. I had already rebooked my departure with the airlines. The cost for rebooking added worry to my already stressful situation.

I received a call from her doctor and the brain specialist. They needed to speak to me. They let me know her brain showed a considerable lack of memory cells and signs of deterioration. Her dementia was most definitely worsening. It would eventually affect her mobility because the communication between her brain and her body was declining rapidly. She also had a heart malfunction that could not be repaired at her age and in her condition. They informed me there was nothing else they could do. They'd seen this pattern many times. She would just continue to have health episodes that would put her back in the hospital over and over again. I could feel my stomach sinking to the basement of my soul. "*I was just with her and she is back to herself,*" I argued, trying to make sense of this diagnosis.

"*That's the medicine giving her temporary relief,*" they explained.

What should I do? I felt like a little boy with no parents to guide me. One option was to return her to the rehabilitation center that she hated. I knew I couldn't do that to her. This was not how her story was going to end. If it was the last thing I did, I would get her back to her assisted living home. I immediately called the owner/director. He said they could not take hospice patients. I told him I felt she was doing fine and she was getting better. He said he would come visit with her and assess her. In the meantime, they sent over a hospice representative. I remember she was very young. I told her I would not sign anything until the director of assisted living assessed her. I told her I was leaving in a few days and had to get this settled. The urgency to meet that plane and return to Kaua`i actually served me in getting her back to her home. It forced me to make decisions quickly.

The assisted living director assessed her and felt it was fine for her to come back home. My plan seemed to be unfolding perfectly. Still, the hospice representative had to change one item on her contract. There was some legal wording that would allow her to go home, but still allow hospice to visit her once a week. I forcefully told that hospice worker I would not sign anything unless she changed the wording. She agreed and my mother was free to go home.

I went to my mother's room and told her what I considered to be good news. *"You'll be able to go back to your home. You won't have to return to the rehab center."*

She was happy, but then she asked me when I was going home. *"In a few days,"* I said as quickly as I could. The room went silent. Like a thief in the night, I went back to the rehab center to pack her things. Thankfully, her troublesome roommate was asleep. I told management she would not be returning and I left, grateful for what was unfolding. I sat in her room at the assisted living home like a lost little boy, knowing I did a good job. This would be her last home and she would have her integrity. My mother's birthday was coming up. It wasn't until July 8, and I was leaving. I wanted to have some kind of celebration before my departure. I invited Elaine and a few other friends to be there.

You might be judging me now for leaving my mother at her time of need. I take some time here to pause and reach back in hindsight. Yes, maybe I should have acted differently. However, it is useless to look at one's past and play out another scenario. In fact, it is sheer torture. All I can do is reframe the experience for myself. I had done what I set out to do – get her home. I felt I definitely would come back before she transitioned. Was I fooling myself? I believe I really thought that would be the case. The doctors said she could last a couple of weeks or a couple of years. They didn't know. Does anyone know when another person will actually die? What made me leave that day? Here is a word from the little boy inside of me.

"Ever since I was a little boy, I was in fear that my mother would be taken from me. Maybe my father would kill her. Maybe my brother would hurt her and maybe even take her life. Maybe she would be killed in a car accident after a party at the Moose Lodge. They drank and drove, after all. If my

mother died, what would happen to me? She was my only sanity, the only hope that I would grow up safely. What if she died and I was left with my father or taken to a home? What if I wasn't a good boy and God decided to punish me and take her away from me. I prayed every day, and I am not exaggerating. Every day I prayed, lit candles, and begged God not to take my mother away from me before I could take care of myself. That is why I became the Little Man. A man is supposed to be able to take care of himself and his family. I negotiated with life. I made deals with God. If I kept my mother happy and safe, she would stay until I could take care of myself."

In my mind, I feel I raised my family. I deserved to grow up and be free to take care of myself. I was now an adult, or so I thought. I believe that this part of me wanted my mother to have everything she desired all the way to the end of her life, but that included me. I could not give her what she wanted and I could not keep her from dying. As I write this book, the realization I am having is I left home at nineteen years old but I never really left home until I decided to go to Kaua'i. In all honesty, the day I got on that plane to return to Kaua'i, after securing my mother in her home and sparing her from dying in that dreaded rehabilitation center, was the day the Little Man came through once again. I gave her everything she needed, except the thing she wanted most – me!

Ironically, walking away was a pattern in my life. I walked away from my father that day in the hospital. My mother and I walked away from my brother before his life support was taken away. I left my brother in other people's hands while he was on a respirator in order to protect my mother from seeing her golden boy take his last breath. I can't help thinking that in this moment, as my mother neared death, the boy who protected her his whole life could not keep her from dying, nor could he standby helplessly watching her die. My days of negotiating with God to keep her alive were over. All I could do was keep her safe. I believe I did just that, to the best of my ability.

It was time for me to return to my home in Hawai'i. I entered Mom's room and said, "*Mom, I am leaving to go back to Kaua'i. I took care of everything so you don't have to go back to that place you hate. You get to go home where you can be comfortable. Does that make you happy Mom?*"

There was a politeness in her demeanor and a surrendering on her part that was new for me. I felt I was ripping out her soul. I did get on the plane that day. It was the eleventh hour when I finally got it all done and saw her safely in her home. I knew it was the right thing to do. And yet, it was not easy and it did not feel good.

I left Elaine in charge. We would communicate by cell phone. Unfortunately, there were others who entered the drama at the end of my mother's life. According to them, I was the devil incarnate for leaving my mother. The only mistake I made was not to come back immediately and kick every one of those people out of her room. They were most definitely interfering with my mother's care. I found out through hospice that many people were trying to make decisions on her behalf. I will spare the readers the cruel and outrageous events that transpired in my mother's final days. I was able to talk to her a few times and we even talked by zoom. She was shutting down and there was nothing I could do about it. It was too late to go back and I would have to live with that decision.

The hospice nurse put her cell phone on speaker so we could have what turned out to be our last conversation. I let her know I could take care of myself now and that I would be okay. I told her I loved her very much. Her last words to me were, "*I love my little boy.*" The Little Man finally became her little boy.

A few days later, I could feel us disconnecting energetically. I could feel how important it was for me to let go of her so she could be free. On July 23rd, 2014 the call came. She was gone. I knew my life would be very different now that my immediate family was gone. There was only me. On a very deep level, I knew I was going to be all right. It was clear that we had all done the best we could. Take flight, Mom!

***

Several years later, I visited the Veteran's Cemetery in San Francisco where my mother was buried right next to my father. As I looked down at the tombstone with both their names on it, I remembered a time I had questioned her about why she would want to be buried with a man who tortured her for most of her life. She merely said, "*The price is right. It's free.*"

Standing on the Precipice of a Great Change

"What if I fall, oh but my darling what if you fly"
  - J.M. BARRIE, FROM PETER PAN

I stand on the precipice of turning sixty-five years old and finishing this book called *The Memoir of the Little Man*; my heroic childhood journey through my father's mental illness, alcohol abuse, PTSD, delusions, and ending with his final diagnosis of paranoid schizophrenia. I have found the prince inside of me by being present in the confusion and chaos of my childhood, earnestly searching for a solution to the madness. It has led me here to this present moment.

As I navigated through the land mines of fear and danger, this Little Man was confused and curious about this thing called his family and his role in it all. This memoir has allowed me to explain many unanswered questions. How did a little boy maneuver through the secret dysfunctional world into which he was born? My conclusion is I came to this planet with a gift of keeping peace and the ability to learn how to mentally survive out of necessity. I grew through and out of my history into the person I am today.

One of the crucial questions I am asked is, did I ever want to run away from it all? The answer is still, "*No!*" As a matter of fact, I protected the family secret ferociously so I would not be taken away. I innately knew that if I was lucky enough to grow up that someday I would be free. I think that was what got me through some of those tough times. My payoff for the darkest moments was my pride in the role I took as protector and the Little Man. It became my motivation for surviving.

There are not always logical explanations for why we act or think the way we do. When I question why some survive childhood trauma and some do not, my answer is we are all unique individualizations of life. It is not the cards we are dealt, but the hand holding those cards.

As I look back, I feel so proud of this Little Man, not because I survived so much danger, but because of the choices I made that assisted me in becoming the man I am today. What were the tools I used to help me through this maze of a childhood and where did I learn them?

Firstly, my childhood imagination allowed me to see beyond what was in front of me. I saw another movie with a different ending and I was determined to make that new movie come true. When I took that baby doll out of the dumpster and imagined I would save him and protect him from being hurt or destroyed, it is clear to me that it was the pure spiritual/psychological genius I possessed. I wrote, directed, acted in, and produced a story that could and did help me believe that I could survive my father, brother, and the terror of my childhood. My love for acting and drive to be an actor allowed me to imagine that I could be someone else in the play called my life. I knew my life was very real, but just like in the movies, it could always have a different ending. My movie had many emotions and I felt them all.

Secondly, I had the tool of my spirituality in the form of

religion. I had unseen friends known as saints to assist me from the heavens. In times of fear, I remember depending on St. Therese of the Little Flower on many occasions. In my religion classes as a young boy, the nuns taught us that St. Therese would send you a rose unexpectedly so you would know she was there helping you. I believed that story and roses did appear. I kept that belief for many years into my adulthood.

Today, I am a spiritual leader. My wife and I founded Center for Spiritual Living Kaua'i on the island of Kaua'i. How ironic that I still believe in an unseen Power. However, now I know it is not up in the heavens somewhere, but right here within me. This is the same Power that navigated a young boy to not just survive, but to thrive. The only difference now is that I pray *from* God, not *to* God.

Thirdly, my humor and the ability to experience all my feelings through the chaos gave me an outlet so that I did not keep it all bottled up inside of me. As a child, I had the gift of taking a horrible situation and finding some light in it. Sometimes, just the absurdity of it all made me laugh. And much to the dismay of the teachers at St. David's, I had a natural way of making other people laugh. Making my mother laugh was my claim to fame. I didn't even allow my brother's disdain for my humor to deter me.

As an adult, I continue to reparent my inner child/the Little Man. I am definitely able to help others to do the same thing. I have no doubt that I am very good at this. I am not shy to say I am passionate about this work. My belief is that many of us have left our inner child behind because we are so busy growing up. That young part of each of us is sometimes screaming for us to notice him/her. Unattended, it surfaces in our lives to block our success in many arenas. I use the technique of *reframing*, *reclaiming*, and *renaming* the traumatic events that took place in my childhood. As I look at the events with new eyes and a new perspective, healing takes place.

For example, you have read the section in this book where I climbed into bed with my drunk and angry father in order to appease him. My job was to calm him so he wouldn't hurt the family. That event was very confusing to me, the young boy. At the same time, I was discovering all the feelings associated with growing up. As I continued to mature, that young boy was left not only with memories, but also with unidentified emotions and many unanswered questions. My young boy wanted to understand the feelings he had and make some sense out of that experience. I utilized inner dialogue with that inner me to reframe what occurred. I asked the Little Man how he felt having the job of appeasing his father. He said, *"I felt important, but I felt dirty, scared, confused, and curious at the physical feeling I was having."*

This is where reparenting comes in. As a caring parent of this younger part of me, I continued to ask questions of him and listen. The answers were clear. This Little Man knew he was protecting his mother by appeasing his father. He realized that he was telling his father what he wanted to hear from his wife. I am still in awe at how that little boy knew to take that approach.

As I mentioned before, the genius of a young boy's survival techniques is incredible to remember and to bear witness to as an adult. What started the healing for me was the moment when I asked, *"If we went back to those times with your father, would you still climb into that bed again when your mother asked you to appease your father?"* Without a beat, the answer was, *"Yes,"* he would. Why? Because he would do anything to help and protect his mother.

I responded from a place of reparenting and loving myself, and said to this young boy inside, "*Do you know what that makes you, my little prince? That makes you a superhero! Do you know how much courage that took to protect your mom? I am so proud of you. I want you to know that you never should have had to be put in that position. I am sorry you ever had to go through that. You are my superhero and I love you! I want to say it again. You should never have had to go through that experience. We should never have had to go through that.*"

There was a reframing of an old scene with a new reclaiming and renaming of the story. From that moment, I continued to heal. Because of this self-dialogue, my story went from shame to understanding and forgiveness of myself. Why forgiveness? When we are children, we have a tendency to blame ourselves or to wonder what we did that allowed the abuse to take place. It was when I gave my father back his responsibility for what he did and his part in it that I started my road to freedom. The Little Man was able to feel his power and was able to free himself from that dark bedroom of confusion and fear.

Please be assured, we are not redoing the past. That would be a false expectation. What reframing and reparenting allows us is to take back our power. In severe cases, we are reclaiming the inner child's soul. A very important part of the healing is to let ourselves know how sorry we are that the event took place at all. It is to let us know we are loveable because we are pure Love that has never been touched by the experience. That is who we truly are, and that never changes. We may have to say it many times to that inner self, but it will eventually be received and heal the deepest part of us.

I always thought my sensitivity was a weakness, but it turned out to be the greatest tool I had. Because of my sensitivity and my intuitive nature, I was able to assess danger and take the necessary steps to assist myself. My intuitive nature was heightened. I became an empath. However, although it worked in my favor as a young child, it is not so beneficial as an adult. I have to be careful as I tend to pick up everyone's feelings and emotions.

I know now that this Little Man was an optimist in the fullest meaning of the word.

> *"Optimism is the ability to balance out negative and positive things in situations, circumstances and people. It is the courage to explore opportunities, where others are blocked by risk and failure, with the belief that the future will be better than the past."*
>
> - How To Incorporate Realistic Optimism into Your Life - Forbeshttps://www.forbes. com › sites › 2021/01/07

I believe I was born with this trait and it was tested quite extensively in my family unit and upbringing. Journaling became a healing tool for me. I felt like the male version of Anne Frank. The library was my safe writing place. In the library, I wouldn't get caught by my brother or father. I hid my journal where they couldn't find it. If they did find it and they read what I had written about them, there would be hell to pay.

There were also self-help books. Even at a young age, I read them. I remember reading a book that talked about how to turn adversity into gold. It helped me to know there was hope. I even wrote the author and told her I was going to be a writer someday and help people using my words. I was a magnet for any books that would help me.

My greatest tool was gratitude. I was always grateful for those moments that were free from fear. I never wasted them. When my father was in the mental institutes, gone on a ship, or the moments he appeared normal for a brief time, I treasured and took advantage of those moments. I celebrated every second of freedom until it was taken away again.

There were also some wonderful people who touched my life and threw me an anchor when I needed it most. There were my friends in school, teachers, and people I don't even remember who said or did the right thing at the perfect time. I talked to all my childhood pets and I told them all my secrets and my fears. And there was my mother, who served as mother and father and my ally during it all. I was grateful for the gift that all these role models gave me. I learned exactly what I did not want to become.

I am grateful for the opportunity to give that Little Man a voice through this memoir and to tell the story from a place of strength. My hope is that this book will serve those who have suffered through their own trauma. It is for the little child who still lives inside us all. I send these words out as a message that it is never too late to be free and live fully in the present. It is never too late to create a future perfect for a prince or princess who will become king or queen of their life.

Giving Me Back to Me

"Home is a place we all must find, child. It's not just a place where you eat or sleep. Home is knowing. Knowing your mind, knowing your heart, knowing your courage. If we know ourselves, we're always home, anywhere."

- LENA HORNE, FROM THE WIZ

My mother made her transition in 2014 and I still find myself sorting out my feelings surrounding her death. I wondered why I could never feel her. That all changed while I was writing this book. It happened when I was in the middle of a Dr. Joe Dispenza meditation. I had an unexpected and vivid vision of my mother. In this vision, she was young. In fact, she was the age of thirty-six, the exact age she was when she gave birth to me. Mom was lying down playing with a baby boy. She looked so happy. The baby was giggling and smiling. She bounced the baby up and down and then she brought him close and kissed him. The scene was so full of joy and her happiness was so evident that I could only smile. In the vision, Mom looked over at me. I suddenly realized that the baby was me. I looked into the eyes of the baby and then I looked back at my mother. The love between my mother and me was present and deep. It washed over the moments of turmoil and anger we had at the time of her death, healing any distance and bringing back the love we had shared for this lifetime. What happened next cracked my heart open wide. She kissed the baby again, slowly and lovingly, and while looking into my eyes, handed him to me.

In that moment, I knew most definitely she was handing me back to myself. As I hesitantly took the baby from my mother, she urged me with her eyes to take him and hold him close. I took my baby self and literally put him in my heart. We melded as one. I felt pure elation.

As I began to come back out of my meditation, I felt a sense of deep relief and healing in my heart. This was the goodbye I had wanted with my mother when she died in 2014. I had grieved for almost eight years over that goodbye that we never experienced. Now there was a moment of completion and a knowing that we had come full circle. As the meditation ended, I opened my eyes. The elation left and I felt a sense of emptiness and a new beginning at the same time. My mother was gone, but her returning me to me gave me a new responsibility. It would be up to me to decide what to do with this beginning.

Afterword

At the publishing of this book, Patrick Feren and I have been together in an intimate relationship for over twenty-five years. We've been married for twenty-two of those years. I know as much about him as any person can know about someone else. We have been through many ups and downs during our years together. We have both struggled to survive and triumphed in many areas of our life individually and collectively. We have experienced a deep spiritual journey together. We have created amazing creative projects together. We have founded a great Spiritual Entity here on the island of Kaua`i and we have overcome many obstacles to bring it to life. We have loved each other deeply. We are best friends.

I have spent the last two years editing this memoir side-by-side with Patrick. It has been both a rewarding and harrowing experience. I did not know many of these stories in the depth and rawness in which they have been explained here. Through this editing process, I have come to have an even deeper respect for this man I call my husband.

As you have read this book, realize that you have entered the inner soul of a person who has traveled into the deep pit of horror and despair, and yet has come out the other side as a compassionate and loving human being. This is because he walks his talk and constantly puts into practice what he writes about in this book.

He is a great teacher. He is a rescuer of the little child in each of us. His technique of rescuing through the reframing, renaming, and reclaiming process includes taking us back again and again to that little part of ourselves until he/she knows safety and full integration. It is not enough to face a trauma once and think it is healed. It is an ongoing process that can never be ignored. If we are willing to take that journey, Patrick is there for us, just as he was there for himself.

As his partner and wife, I am more loved and accepted than I have ever been in a relationship. When we got married on July 1, 2001, we pledged to each other we would always change. He has supported the changes that have taken place within me with his whole heart. I do the same for him.

I can testify that this book has changed him, yet again. His openness and honesty have catapulted him to another level of deepness in his own ability to love himself, to love me, and to love others.

I am so grateful for the opportunity to be part of this new journey of unfoldment of the man called Patrick Feren. I know this book will assist so many who read it, but only if they are willing to explore its content in relationship to themselves with perseverance and self-love.

BLESSINGS,
RITA ANDRIELLO-FEREN

Made in the USA
Columbia, SC
11 May 2024

35237139R00135